OUT OF THE
DARKNESS

OUT OF THE
DARKNESS

A JOURNEY INTO THE

LIGHT

Gary,
I Truly miss seeing
your BEAUTiFul selF
Around Here AT work.
You ARE A Blessing in our Lives.
Keep The FAITH And I PRAY
The Lord will HEAL your BODY!

MARK WHITTINGTON

Mark Whittington

TATE PUBLISHING & *Enterprises*

Published by Tate Publishing & Enterprises, LLC
127 E. Trade Center Terrace | Mustang, Oklahoma 73064 USA
1.888.361.9473 | www.tatepublishing.com

Tate Publishing is committed to excellence in the publishing industry. The company reflects the philosophy established by the founders, based on Psalm 68:11,
"The Lord gave the word and great was the company of those who published it."

Book design copyright © 2009 by Tate Publishing, LLC. All rights reserved.
Cover design by Joey Garrett
Interior design by Nathan Harmony

Published in the United States of America

ISBN: 978-1-60696-884-0
Religion: Christian Life: Personal Growth
09.09.15

Again therefore Jesus spoke to them, saying, "I am the light of the world; he who follows Me shall not walk in darkness, but shall have the light of life."

John 8:12

Acknowledgements

I wish to express my gratitude to the following without whom this book would have never become a reality:

To Jesus Christ for dying on the cross for me and allowing me to finally realize that I needed His love.

To my parents for trying to teach me about the Lord, by taking me to Sunday school and church even though many times I did not want to attend. They reached out to help my first marriage by asking a minister to come by to offer his help. They knew the kind of help we needed.

To Walt, the minister that came by my home with the love of Jesus Christ in his heart to offer us help in my first marriage. He offered to share the love and the wisdom of the Lord with us. I had to find out more about the minister and the Lord. This time I allowed the Lord came into my life; I took time to reflect and realized what I had been missing.

To my first wife, Pam, it was my relationship with her that brought me to Jesus, which was a blessing.

To my father-in-law, Charlie, whom I witnessed becoming a better person because he found the love of Jesus Christ. His love and kindness gave me strength when I needed it most. He showed me unconditional love because Jesus was in his heart.

To Kelly Anne, my wife, for loving the Lord first, then loving me and giving me a beautiful son, for her patience and understanding when I lost my focus in the Lord, for her forgiveness when I hurt her, and for her support while writing this story. She is a blessing from the Lord. She has shown me a wife's godly love.

To my son, Matt, who is a big joy in my life and is a blessing from the Lord. I pray that when he is older, he will read this story and learn from it. I pray that he grows to love the Lord.

To Letha Fleming, my sister in law, for working closely with me and for helping bring the pictures together for the book.

To Linda Buzbee, Nan Austin and Monique Bowman, these spirit filled women who have dedicated their lives to teaching made the book stronger through their spiritual awareness and technical expertise.

To Noell Rogers (uncle) for spending many hours to edit and look at each word to make sure the writing and meaning was correct. His spiritual foundation and insight gave me ideas to make many of my spiritual thoughts even stronger.

To Mrs. Ann Self my Sunday school teacher who gave me encouragement, love and her prayers.

To Marie Barber for her artistic gift and spirit filled life that enabled her to complete the beautiful oil painting of Jesus.

Chapters

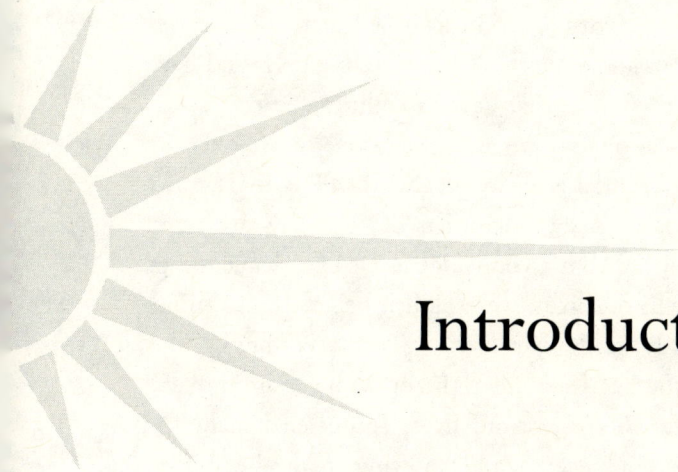

Introduction

This is a true story; it is based on memories of my life from the age of three years. Some of the names were changed to ensure privacy. These experiences have impacted and shaped my life so dramatically that I want to share my passionate faith and the experiences that have brought me to where I am now. I know I have been a recipient of God's unfaltering love, and He extends that love to all of His children.

When I was a young man, I fell to my knees in excruciating mental anguish and asked for the Lord's help. At the time, I felt I had no one in my life. I was confused because my life was not going like I had planned. Once I turned to our Lord, I found His love to be compassionate and understanding. He began to show me why I had not been able to live life as I expected. He brought me peace along with giving me a clearer understanding of myself and others. During that time He placed in my heart a desire to share His story with you. At this time I share these stories with a joyous and open spirit because through Him I have learned many things that have brought me peace, knowledge, and happiness. We are never alone in life once we realize Jesus Christ is always near and willing to listen.

Our earthly makeup consists of our body, our mind and our spirit. From a young age as we experience things that occur in our lives, we establish beliefs in our mind; these beliefs guide our spirit to act accordingly. Our actions, whether they are right or wrong, can and will affect us for the rest of our lives. Too often I made the wrong decisions even while knowing in my heart they were wrong. I knew I could do things better or make a better choice for myself which would improve my quality of life. I could not understand why my mind would not allow this to happen. In my case, a heartbreaking experience triggered an understanding; my spirit awakened to something new—the truth about life. Through this experience I learned that I must listen to my heart, become a disciple of the Lord, have the faith to enter the narrow gate of heaven, and change my worldly ways.

> *For all that is in the world, the lust of the flesh and the lust of the eyes and the boastful pride of life, is not from the Father, but is from the world.*
>
> I John 2:16

> *And do not be conformed to this world, but be transformed by the renewing of your mind, that you*

> *may prove what the will of God is, that which is good*
> *and acceptable and perfect.*
>
> Romans 12:2

What are the ways of the world? There are many verses
in the Bible that reference the world and worldly ways.
When I refer to worldly ways I am referring to self-centeredness; our focus is on ourselves, not others. We strive
to acquire more material things no matter how we achieve
them; we depend on other people for our happiness, and
we try to find happiness in things we do instead of first
placing our faith in the Lord. While striving for happiness, we often rationalize and justify our actions when we
are wrong. Do our minds deceive us? Without the Lord
in our lives we can be like a storm that is destructive to
ourselves and others. Deep down there is a sense of emptiness; something is missing. We want to feel peace, but
we don't know how to find it. We are always reaching for
something to fulfill our lives, but cannot find it. The Lord
calls this *walking in darkness*. There are things that can
only be attained through Jesus Christ. God gives us grace
when we accept Jesus Christ as our Savior, and when we
walk with the Lord, we strive to act with integrity; when
we make a commitment, we follow through. We are concerned how our actions will affect others. The center of
our lives becomes focused on Jesus and not on ourselves.
If we walk with Him, He will bless us. The Lord calls this
walking in the light. Darkness cannot overcome the smallest ray of light. Look up in the sky on a pitch-black night,
and sometimes you will only see one star. Notice the huge

expanse of sky and the tiny speck of light. What catches your eye, the darkness of night or the beauty of the small shining star? God is the Light. In the end, the Light will rule and be judgment; Light will prevail.

> *Again therefore Jesus spoke to them, saying, "I am the light of the world; he who follows Me shall not walk in darkness, but shall have the light of life."*
>
> John 8:12

> *In the beginning was the Word, and the Word was with God, and the Word was God. He was in the beginning with God. All things came into being by Him, and apart from Him nothing came into being that has come into being. In Him was life, and the life was the light of men. And the light shines in the darkness, and the darkness did not comprehend it.*
>
> John 1:1–5

If you open your heart to the Lord when reading my story, you will find answers to questions about life for which you have been searching. My story will show you how to accept Jesus Christ as your Savior and to find peace and the light of knowledge with the certainty of having eternal life with our Lord. If you are unsure that you are good enough to be recognized at the heavenly gates, you will also find the answer in my story. Do you want the best for yourself, your family, and your children?

With an open heart, read the Bible verses below; this can be a new beginning, giving you the right foundation to begin change in your life or strengthen your faith. You do not have to experience the pain I did before you open your heart to the Lord's word, the spirit of *Lightness*. We learn from the word that the Light of life reminds us to be aware of vanity (boasting), carnality (fleshly wars), praying (for ourselves & others), and peace (reconciliation).

Yet you do not know what your life will be like tomorrow. You are just a vapor that appears for a little while and then vanishes away. Instead, you ought to say, "If the Lord wills, we shall live and also do this or that." But as it is, you boast in your arrogance; all such boasting is evil.

James 4:14–16

For we know that the Law is spiritual; but I am of flesh, sold into bondage to sin. For that which I am doing, I do not understand; for I am not practicing what I would like to do, but I am doing the very thing I hate. But if I do the very thing I do not wish to do, I agree with the Law, confessing that it is good.

Romans 7:14–16

And I know that when I come to you, I will come in the fullness of the blessing of Christ. Now I urge, you brethren, by our Lord Jesus Christ and by the love of the spirit, to strive together with me in your prayers to God for me.

Romans 15:29–30

Therefore if any man is in Christ, he is a new creature; the old things passed away; behold, new things have come. Now all these things are from God, who reconciled us to Himself through Christ, and gave us the ministry of reconciliation,

II Corinthians 5:17–18

Therefore, gird your minds for action, keep sober in spirit, fix your hope completely on the grace to be brought to you at the revelation of Jesus Christ. As obedient children, do not be conformed to the former lusts which were your ignorance, but like the Holy One called you, be holy yourselves also in all your behavior; because it is written, "You Shall Be Holy, For I Am Holy."

I Peter 1:13–16

For from within, out of the heart of men, proceed the evil thoughts, fornications, thefts, murders, adulteries, deeds of coveting and wickedness, as well as deceit, sensuality, envy, slander, pride and foolishness. "All these evil things proceed from within and defile the man."

Mark 7:21–23

To find a life of peace and maintain our *Light,* we must be cognizant that our flesh can be overcome only by attaining a constant and consistent communion with the spirit which is given for each of us at all times.

The Appearance

I would like to share a powerful experience I had with Jesus when I was nine years old. My parents had a picture of Jesus hanging in the small hallway leading into the den of our home. The den had a glass doll case sitting at an angle across from the picture. One night it was unusually stormy with cascading thunder and awesome lightening. The noise of the thunder and the torrential downpour woke me. I was shaking with fright, so, I went to the den and curled up in one of the chairs. The large, comfortable chair had always made me feel safe and protected. The storm was ferocious and shook the windows with wind whistling around the whole house.

Just when I was feeling the whole house would be blown away, I saw someone standing in front of the glass doll case.

At first, I thought it was the reflection of the picture of Jesus; however, I couldn't see the picture from where I was sitting. The image was calming and resembled the picture of Jesus, but was somehow different. The man standing in front of me looked like he was made of mist, and as I continued to stare at him; it appeared as though he was blanketed in a thick coat of fog and that I was seeing him from a distance. The image was more than the reflection of a man's bust hanging from the wall in our hallway. I saw his full form, from his long hair and beard to his sandaled feet. Finally he spoke to me. He said, "I am Jesus Christ and you are a disciple of Mine. Your name is Mark." At the sound of his voice, I felt calm. His voice spoke with confidence. I could tell He was a caring person. I was curious if this was really happening to me. As I reached out to touch Him, the vapor of mist vanished as mysteriously as He had appeared to me. Moments after Jesus disappeared I smelled a musty odor in the room. The smell reaffirmed that I was not dreaming about His appearance.

At the time, I did not have the knowledge to understand what Jesus was saying to me, nor was I confident enough to talk to my parents about what I had seen and heard. Over the years, I placed that memory in storage, but deep down in my soul I never forgot Jesus coming to me.

Years later, as an adult, experiencing the greatest pain I had ever known, Jesus again spoke to me through my heart and soul. I began to think about His visit to me as a child. As I relived the memory of that night, Jesus appeared to me; I clearly remembered his facial details along with the robe He was wearing and His sandaled feet. His arms were open in a loving manner. He was an ordinary man. He had spoken to me and had known my name then, just as He now knew my name during the suffering and pain that was to follow me years later. How did Jesus know me? I am a creation of God, and He knows every one by name.

> *Indeed, the very hairs of your head are all numbered. Do not fear; you are of more value than many sparrows. And I say to you, everyone who confesses Me before men, the Son of Man shall confess him also before the angels of God; but he who denies Me before men shall be denied before the angels of God.*
>
> Luke 12:7–9

Jesus Christ is real, and the Bible is nothing but the truth. Please open your heart to the Lord as you read my story. I pray that you are blessed with the love and wisdom of the Lord. If you place my story in your heart and think about what I am saying, you will see that the true way of life is through Jesus Christ. There is no doubt Jesus wants me to share His appearance that stormy night with you. I hope by my sharing my encounter with Jesus, your faith becomes stronger, and that you know He is alive today. His arms are open to love us all no matter what path we have taken in life.

> *Jesus said to him, I am the way, and the truth, and the life; no one comes to the Father, but through Me. If you had known Me, you would have known My Father also; from now on you know Him, and have seen Him.*
>
> John 14:6–7

For Christ also died for sins once for all, the just for the
unjust, in order that He might bring us to God, having
been put to death in the flesh, but made alive in the spirit.

I Peter 3:18

I know it is difficult for people to just accept what I am
telling them. I was a skeptic once, too. Over the years, I
have questioned why or even whether Jesus came to me
during that storm. I now truly believe that He did, and
that He wanted me to follow a particular path, His path
which I ignored for too many years. After His death on
the cross, Jesus appeared to His disciples on a mountain
near Galilee to relieve their doubts, to lessen their pain,
and to comfort them. He assured them that He was still
alive. They must still go on in life, but live with His spirit
in their hearts. They must go out into the world and share
His love, making disciples of others.

But the eleven disciples proceeded to Galilee, to the
mountain which Jesus had designated. And when they saw
Him, they worshipped Him; but some were doubtful. And
Jesus came up and spoke to them, saying, All authority has
been given to Me in heaven and on earth. Go therefore and
make disciples of all nations, baptizing them in the name
of the Father and the Son and the Holy Spirit, teaching
them to observe all that I commanded you; and lo, I am
with you always, even to the end of the age.

Matthew 28:16–20

Once I accepted Jesus Christ as my Savior, I started to
read the Bible; I began to understand more about God

and His Spirit that changed my perspective about life. Over the years I have heard the Trinity mentioned in Christian topics. The Trinity is described as the unity of God the Father, Jesus Christ the Son and the Holy Spirit as three persons who have the same essence of deity (Divine Being). The Trinity is a complex topic to understand. Why would God inspire the use of the plural pronouns "Us" and "Our" as found in Genesis 1:26 unless He was revealing that the three comes from Him.

> *Then God said, "Let Us make man in Our image, according to Our likeness; and let them rule over the fish of the sea and over the birds of the sky and over the cattle and over all the earth, and over every creeping thing that creeps on earth." And God created man in His own image, in the image of God He created him; male and female He created them. And God blessed them; and God said to them, "Be fruitful and multiply, and fill the earth, and subdue it; and rule over, the fish of the sea and over the birds of the sky, and over every living thing that moves on the earth."*
>
> Genesis 1:26–28

The Trinity gives us our God for all times–past, present and future. Not only do these manifestations of the God head imbue us with power, Christ in His power brought and still brings us with power, Christ in His power brought and still brings wholeness to our lives.

Many times in the Bible, I have read about Jesus healing someone. I know His healing power can forgive me for my sins. Many of us are lost in the world and do not have the Lord in our hearts, perhaps, because many have never been told the truth about Jesus, or they have not taken time to realize the truth about Him. Marriages are failing too often. Children are being physically, mentally, and sexually abused. Many children are not getting the support they need from their parents because their parents do not have the Lord as their spiritual foundation. Change can happen in our lives; our perception toward life can change. Often the change we need comes from within our hearts.

In my heart I know Jesus wants me to tell His story. He is real, and the Bible is the truth. Hearts can be changed with Jesus Christ's love. He wants to love you. You can be a disciple for the Lord. We need to share with people that Jesus is real and the Bible is the truth about life. The sharing begins at home.

Jesus' Appearance that Stormy Night
Artist Marie Barber

Thoughts for Reflection

- Jesus Christ is real, and the Bible is the truth. God loves us all. You have a choice to make: to accept His love or not.

- God wants us to share our experiences of His love with others. I truly hope you take my experience of Jesus appearing to me to heart while it strengthens your faith. Jesus is real even in today's times.

- Sometimes we try to change our outer appearance so we can feel better about ourselves. Often we just need a change of our heart to be happy. God changes hearts.

- God can give you the wisdom to choose living in His lightness. Just ask Him.

- Jesus appeared to me for only a few moments. Our lives on earth are like moments compared to our life in eternity.

Bible Verses for Study

In the beginning God created the heavens and the earth.

Genesis 1:1

Jesus therefore was saying to those Jews who had believed in Him, "If you abide in My word, then you are truly disciples of Mine; and you shall know the truth, and the truth shall make you free.

John 8:31–32

Trust in the Lord with all your heart, And do not lean on your own understanding.

Proverbs 3:5

And as for these four youths, God gave them knowledge and intelligences in every branch of literature and wisdom; Daniel even understood all kinds of visions and dreams,

Daniel 1:17

Although He was a Son, He learned obedience from the things He suffered. And having made perfect, He became to all those who obey Him the source of eternal salvation.

Hebrews 5:8–9

Let it be known to all of you, and to all the people of Israel, that by the name of Jesus Christ the Nazarene, whom you crucified, whom God raised from the dead-by this name this man stands here before you in good health. "He is the stone which was rejected by you, the builders, but which became the very corner stone. "And there is salvation in no one else; for there is no other name under heaven that has been given among men, by which we must be saved."

Acts 4:10–12

Jesus answered, "The foremost is, 'Hear, O Israel! The Lord our God is one Lord; and you shall love the Lord your God with all your heart, and with all your soul, and with all your mind and with all your strength.' "The second is this, 'You shall love your neighbor as yourself.' There is no other commandment greater than these."

Mark 12:29–31

Questions

1. Why did Jesus die on the cross?

2. Why is it important to follow the Lord and do His will?

3. What happens to our spirit when we accept Jesus into our heart?

4. What memories have you placed in storage that could be shared or hidden issues that need to be dealt with?

What Do
Children Feel?

Even as an infant I was aware of the feelings of love and the feelings of rejection. I believe all babies and children instinctively know when they are loved or unloved. Most parents will affirm that children respond to love and retreat from rejection. Throughout our lives we are constantly looking for acceptance and love; we do not like rejection. My goal is to show how to live a rich and fulfilling life by putting Jesus at the center, knowing and feeling His love and His acceptance. His love is the greatest of all. I would like to share with you how God began showing me about lightness and darkness at around the age of four years old. The Bible uses the concept of *light* and *dark*.

From my perspective light represents God's love and His ways while dark represents rejection, being lost, our sins, and uncertainty about life.

I lived with my birth parents for only a short period of time. My mother was very young and was dating an older man when she became pregnant with me. They married, and the three of us moved into a trailer. From the beginning my parents were always yelling and scream-ing at each other. As soon as a fight started, they would tell me to go outside and play. Sometimes it was pitch black in the middle of the night, and I remember being very scared. I would hide behind a big oak tree looking back at the small light over the outside door of the trailer, and then I would hug the big tree in our yard, hoping they would let me come back in soon. I felt so alone and unprotected. As I hugged the tree, I would look back at the tiny light because it gave me an undefined peace and security that I was not alone. All I could think about was who or what was going to come and carry me away or hurt me. The time I spent in the darkness felt like an eter-nity to me. I was only about four years old. Was God try-ing to show me at such a young age about darkness and light? Sometime during that time, the state took me away from my parents and sent me to a foster home … and then another … and then another. At times I would stay with my grandmother. I had no place I could call home.

I remember being in two foster homes before I was adopted. The first one had four children, and I was so excited because I would have real kids to play with, not just imaginary ones. I finally had an older brother that I could look up to. However, it wasn't long before the excitement gave way to a new fear. One day my new brother tried to run away from home. He was walking down the road when his dad caught him. To keep him from running away again, his dad tied his hands with a rope and put him into the truck. When they got home, his dad dragged him into the house, leading him with the rope. He took him into the bedroom and tied his feet and arms to each corner of the bed. The boy was lying on his stomach naked. A familiar fear started to creep through me. Even though his dad had closed the door, I was still able to peek through a crack. I saw his dad beat him with a strap. All the while his mother sobbed silently. I knew this was some kind of warning and that things would not get better. I hoped it would not happen to me. This new fear of physical harm was terrifying.

At one point during my stay with this family, all of the children, including myself, were taken to a cotton field and told to pick cotton until the bag was full. We were told we could not have anything to drink until our bag was full. I held the bag up in the air with both hands as high as I could and realized half of the bag was still touching the ground. I knew I was in trouble; I could die of thirst and hunger before I filled the bag. I had never picked cotton before, and I remember the pain as the sharp points of the dried cotton burs cut and bloodied my tender hands. I was terrified of my foster dad and kept my distance from him. I knew I could never get close to him, but I was able to show the children my love because like me they were still innocent about life. We truly did not understand at such a young age the cruelties of life that could come to us.

Cotton Boll

The next foster home had no children, and the couple was much older. I was hesitant about walking into their home with my suitcase because I didn't know what to expect. Their house was damp, cold, and dreary looking. They led me to my room and closed the bedroom door. After they left, I sat on the bed thinking I would have to try and run away. There couldn't possibly be any love in this house. I checked the bedroom window to see if I could escape from this cold house. I would run back to my other foster home where there were children that loved me or to my grandmother's home. After a few minutes, I realized that I couldn't run away because I really had nowhere to go. I sat down on the bed and cried because I felt that no one loved me. There was no one I could depend on. That was the loneliest I had ever felt. I was alone in the world. What I did not realize, yet, was that God was with me every step of the way.

I had the good fortune to spend time living with my grandmother before I was finally adopted. I remember the love I felt from my grandmother. She was old and full of wisdom, but her health was poor. I could tell she loved me. She would cook homemade apple pies for me and place them on the open window ledge in the kitchen. Then she would tell me to go play while they cooled. I loved her apple pies and would ask every few minutes if the pie was cool enough to eat. Finally, I would get to eat a big piece. She wanted to care for me, but her health was failing, and she could no longer keep me. It got to the point where no one in my birth family would take care of me properly, and so the state came again to take me away from my family. I remember waiting with a little suitcase in one hand and my beloved stuffed bunny in the other.

Before I left my family for the last time, my mom said good-bye to me and told me that she was so sorry to have to let me go. She put a small Bible in my hands. Years later, when I was a teenager, my adopted mom gave me the Bible. Inside it my birth mom had written: *To my little boy on his 4th birthday, Love Mommie.*

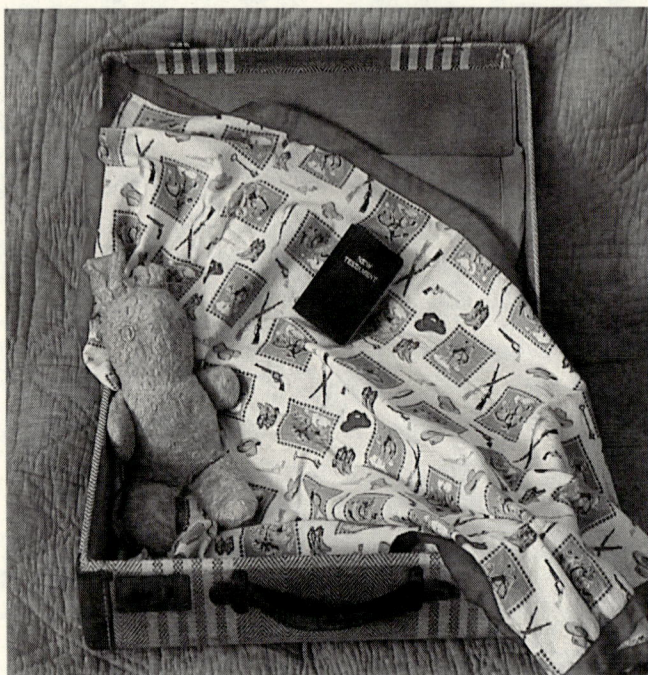

My Few Earthly Possessions

Finally, a family that wanted a son found me and wanted to love me. They adopted me right before my fifth birthday. My new parents were a wonderful couple. They had an adopted daughter that was then ten years old. I could tell that they were all overjoyed to get me. I was like a prize they were showing off to other family members and friends. Having that much attention was a very happy time in my life. I finally had a loving home! I knew growing up in their family that they cared for me and wanted the best for me.

During the adoption process, my adoptive parents

were told by the legal authorities that I was capable of finishing high school, but would not be able to attend a regular four-year college. My adoptive parents accepted the schooling issue and tried very hard to support me in school. They never expected me to go to college. To their surprise I did finish college. Because of my work ethic over the years, I have been very successful from a materialistic viewpoint. However, I have realized that material things do not make me happy. What makes me happy and brings me peace in life is being loved, and sharing that love with Jesus in my heart. Sharing the love of Jesus is true happiness because that is what He wants us to do.

Over the years, I have met married couples like my adoptive parents that could not have children. They were very special people. I could tell they were disappointed because their hopes and dreams of having a family together were not going as planned. I would tell them that I was adopted and would ask them if they had considered adopting a child. Their answer would be that they had thought about it but would probably not act on it. I tried to encourage them to reconsider adoption. They had love and a home to give, and there are children who need that love and would return it and fulfill their dreams. Taking a child no one else wants or a child that a family cannot support and giving that child love will bring more love in return than they ever thought possible. I was able to overcome adversity in my life because of the teaching of my adopted family. I believe that God sent me to them.

Every one of us is a result of Gods creative work. Each one of us is special in His eyes. He wants us to love Him as our heavenly Father. All young children long to be loved and know what love is because we are God's children. Do you long to be loved and accepted by someone? Is your heart missing the love of God? Is your child looking out the window wishing to be loved by you? At the young age of four, God was reaching out to me when I was in the darkness hugging the big tree; I did not realize it until years later.

Thoughts for Reflection

- God created all of us in His image. We have a choice to follow Him as a child of His. Each one of us is special in His eyes.

- Listen and watch. You may learn something even from a child.

- When I was younger, I took everything so seriously. I had a hard time laughing. We have opportunities to laugh every day. Laughter will make us a more fun person to be around. It is wiser to learn this at a young age. I enjoy hearing the laughter of a child.

- As children grow, they have many dreams. If you have children, help them be realistic in how to accomplish their dreams. Our dreams begin with God and with His help we can accomplish them.

Bible Verses for Study

For God so loved the world, that He who gave His only begotten Son, that whoever believes in Him should not perish, but have eternal life. For God did not send the Son into the world to judge the world, but that the world should be saved through Him. He who believes in Him is not judged; he who does not believe has been judged already, because he has not believed in the name of the only begotten Son of God. And this is the judgment, that the light is come into the world, and men loved the darkness rather than the light; for their deeds were evil. For everyone who does evil hates the light, and does not come to the light, lest his deeds should be exposed. But he who practices the truth comes to the light, that his deeds may be manifested as having been wrought in God."

John 3:16–21

The end of all things is at hand; therefore, be sound judgment and sober spirit for the purpose of prayer. Above all, keep fervent in your love for one another, because love covers a multitude of sins.

I Peter: 4:7–8

And this is the message we have heard from Him and announce to you, God is light, and in Him there is no darkness at all. If we say that we have fellowship with Him and yet walk in the darkness, we lie and do not practice the truth; but if we walk in the light as He himself is in the light, we have fellowship with one another, and the blood of Jesus His son cleanses us from all sin.

I John 1:5–7

Questions

1. When was the first time you felt being loved and felt totally rejected by someone not loving you?

2. How do you feel when you are in the darkness by yourself?

3. Do you remember any cruelties of life you faced at a young age? If so, have you been able to forgive the people or person that hurt you?

4. Do you feel God loves you at all times in your life?

5. Have you every felt or wondered why you could not find someone to love you?

6. All throughout the Bible God has directed people to write about Love. Love your neighbor, love your enemy, love the sinner, etc. Why is love so important to God?

7. God created us in His image. What image should we carry or portray in our lives?

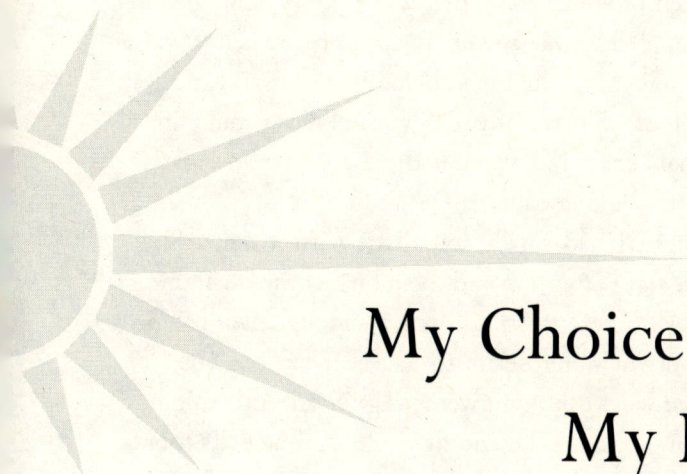

My Choice for My Life

Faith in God helps one make the right choices in all phases of life. Even when choosing the person with whom you want to spend the rest of your life. Unfortunately, I chose to let my emotions take control, and, as a result, I married a woman who was not committed to a lifelong relationship. Her main focus was herself. God tried to show me this during our dating relationship, but I was not open to hearing Him. My insecurities and need to be loved blinded me to almost everything except "love" as I perceived it. I did not listen to my heart; God was telling me, *Do not marry her.* I did not want to understand what He was saying, and I did not care to listen. I was focused only on myself.

Things never worked out with the girls I dated in high school even though I thought I was a pretty good guy. I treated people the way I would want to be treated. I was the co-captain of the high school football team and an all-star state football player my senior year. I never could find that special person to love me—that is, until Pam walked into my life while in college.

I thought I had finally found the perfect mate. She gave me a lot of attention and spent quality time with me. It wasn't long before we fell into a serious relationship. In my overwhelming desire to have her be "the one," I overlooked what I thought were insignificant little things, such as an occasional lie and her jealousy. I actually took her jealousy as a compliment. After so many years of longing for someone to care for me, her love brought exquisite joy. We dated for one and a half years while in college, and we talked about marriage. We became engaged with plans to marry when we graduated. I knew in my heart our relationship was not totally right. Even before we were married, I had doubts. Was God speaking to me?

I did talk to Pam about my concerns, but she dismissed them by saying that getting married would give her the security she needed. I wanted to believe her and did not want to lose her love. I walked down the aisle, and we were married. I did not listen to what God was trying to tell me. Once we became man and wife, we became more relaxed and our true selves became evident. Our home situation was not a happy one. There was a lot of tension in our relationship.

One of the things I chose not to notice before we were married were the conflicts Pam caused in our friends' lives.

When we moved into our first apartment, we met a nice couple that tried to take us under their wings, and show us the area. They had grown up there and knew everyone. Leslie was a fireman who was overweight by several hundred pounds, and his wife was very small and attractive. He was a kind, caring man and would help anyone. Over the next few months, we spent time with Leslie and Susan. One day Leslie came to me almost in tears saying that Pam had made comments to his wife that she could not see how his wife loved him because of his appearance. I told him how sorry I was that that had happened. That was the end of that relationship. I asked Pam about this, and she said that his wife had misunderstood what she was saying. I accepted her explanation. Over the next 4-½ years, we met other couples, but no one stayed friends with us for long. Pam drove away our friends with her cutting remarks and by creating conflicts with her demands. Even in public, she insulted and demeaned waitresses and cashiers. I was confused by her actions since I had never noticed this behavior in her before. I did not understand why she treated people in this manner. I was taught by my parents to care for all people. I would drive down the road and wave to anybody I met on the highway. One day we were driving home, and I waved to someone I didn't know, and Pam asked me in a cutting way why I did that. I said I did so because it was a nice thing to do. Over time I stopped waving to people because of her remarks. I allowed her to influence my stopping what I considered to be a good deed. Even though I felt I was giving Pam all the emotional support I could allow myself under the circumstances, I did not receive any similar encouragement from her.

The lies were coming more frequently, and I confronted her. She dismissed them with more lies. Acquaintances accused her of being unfaithful to me on several occasions, which she denied. This broke my heart even though I was not able to find out the truth. All this started less than a year after we were married. My hopes, my dreams and my heart were being shattered. I searched for the truth because I had lost faith in Pam. It was difficult for me to accept that anyone would accuse her of adultery if it weren't true. Everyone, supposedly involved, denied all wrongdoing.

From that point on I started watching Pam closer. The lies and accusations were taking a toll on me and on our relationship. The lies were bad; many became almost ridiculous and cruel. Then one day, I knew she was being unfaithful and confronted her. This time she could not deny the truth even though she tried to lie her way out of it. My wife, the person that I loved the most, had deceived me and broken my heart. I immediately felt somehow responsible. What had I done that was so bad that I deserved this kind of treatment? The betrayal and pain was almost unbearable. I questioned why Pam had wanted to marry me from the beginning. During my marriage I lost my self-confidence and my trust in her. I felt I was on the verge of a nervous breakdown. Why was my life turning out this way? I couldn't eat nor sleep. I tortured myself by dwelling on each lie and betrayal. I couldn't understand why she felt she had to lie. I questioned what kind of person could be so cold hearted. I was full of questions and hurt. Finally, I tried to understand why I should want to stay married to Pam. All I could think about was that marriage was a commitment for life. I did not want a change in my life even though my situation was almost unbearable.

> *Let us behave properly as in the day, not in carousing and drunkenness, not in sexual promiscuity and sensuality, not in strife and jealousy. But put on the Lord Jesus Christ, and make no provision for the flesh in regard to its lusts.*
>
> Romans 13: 13–14

I told Pam she needed to decide if she wanted to be married to me. It was her decision to make whether she wanted a divorce. I did not want a divorce. All I wanted was for her to love me and to be honest. I realized I could not live this way any longer. She convinced me that she loved me and wanted to stay married. She said that she had made a mistake.

My love for her eventually became a reflection of her love for me. In reality, the changes in me began from the beginning of our relationship. I was no longer the person I used to be. I had allowed her kind of love to transform me into a jealous, insecure person, which made both of our lives miserable. I could not find a way to forgive her. We didn't know how to live our lives together.

Slowly, I began to withdraw because I was scared that our marriage would not last. I had no idea what it would take to repair the damage to the marriage and my heart; I was running on emotions. The hurt was almost unbearable. While I did not understand what was happening to our relationship; I knew that something had to change. I knew I did not want to live our lives together like this. I was lost in my misery not knowing what to do. I was lost not having the spiritual understanding I needed in my life. I knew about commitment in a marriage because of my parents' example. I knew about morals and values, but I did not see these things in my marriage. I tried to trust her again. I felt I had no one to talk to about what was going on in our lives except for Pam.

As time progressed, I thought our relationship was getting better. We were talking through some issues. I had encouraged her to do something constructive for herself, something that would give her some self-esteem. She seemed excited and decided to go back to school to become a nurse. While we were dating in college, she had decided school was not for her at the time. She did not finish school. Should this have been a danger sign to me about her commitment to stay with me or finish something she began? We also decided to try and have a child while she was in school, which was exciting. The last few weeks before school was out for break, she said that she had to write a paper about someone special in her life. I was devastated when she said that she did not know anyone that was special enough to write about. She continued to say things especially designed to indicate that I was not special in her heart. After several weeks of remarks like this, I realized that that she had given up on our marriage.

To break the routine, I suggested we go out bowling and to a bar with two of our remaining friends. We were in the bar for less than ten minutes before she started saying that certain guys looked really "good" to her. I felt she was trying to hurt me. She was trying to hurt me. It worked because I was sick from the pain and humiliation. I walked out of the bar without her. I thought about leaving her there to find her own way back home. In a few minutes, she came out with our friends. We ended up leaving together. We made it home, and my heart was about to burst from the hurt. I asked myself why she would be so cruel to me with her comments. I again questioned myself about the kind of person I had married.

> *An excellent wife is the crown of her husband, but she who shames him is as rottenness in his bones.*
>
> Proverbs 12:4

> *One of the six things the Lord Hates is haughty eyes, a lying tongue.*
>
> Proverbs 6:17

In the early part of our marriage when we got into an argument or fight, we would put aside the words and make love. I thought making love would help us feel close again. Now, I asked her to make love on several occasions. I begged her to love me, and she refused. All I wanted to do was make things better between us. Then, one night, I sexually forced myself on her. I actually thought that by forcing the act of love, it would make the situation better. This was a big mistake. I should have taken the initiative and ended the marriage. I hated the things we did to each other. We were cruel to each other. At that time I had no one with whom to share my feelings. Our friends were no longer around, and I felt isolated. I did not have a spiritual relationship with the Lord. I was lost. There was no one to turn to for help.

> *I said to myself concerning the sons of men, "God has surely tested them in order for them to see that they are but beasts.*
>
> Ecclesiastes 3:18

Pam did not leave after that terrible night, but she started talking about leaving me again. She had left before, but for some reason she always came back after a time of separation. Things would get better between us. This time I knew things were different, so I reached out to my mom and dad. I had never asked for help before. My parents knew what help our marriage needed, so they sent a minister to our house one night. Walt, the minister, offered to counsel us. He said he would show us how a marriage could work by placing God at the center. I was excited that finally we could learn how to be a married couple, but Pam was not interested. She left and went back home to her dad.

Has a Stranger Made the Effort to Help You or Share God's Love?

Thoughts for Reflection

- Good and bad decisions we make can affect the rest of our lives.

- Beware of people who lie. There is never only one lie.

- Do not hesitate to ask someone to help you when issues arise in any part of your life. If you wait, it could be too late to get help.

- If you have a personal relationship with God, people will see Him in you.

- When I was younger I thought I had answers to life and thought I knew about life until I had to face adversity. I realized I knew nothing about life until I asked God for His help and felt His love. Be confident in God's ability to guide you; if you guide yourself you will fail.

- People are often good at telling you what you want to hear, but never follow through with their commitment or what they say they are going to do. Do they just have good intentions while not following through, or do they realize they just lie?

- Get to know someone before you give your love and heart to them. If they do not have the love of God in their heart and soul, they may damage your heart forever.

Bible Verses for Study

Do not judge lest you be judged. For the way you judge, you will be judged. And by your standard of measure, it will be measured to you. And why do you look at the speck that is in your brother's eye, but do not notice the log that is in your own eye?

Matthew 7:1–3

And just as you want people to treat you, treat them in the same way.

Luke 6:31

For the lips of an adulteress drip honey, and smoother than oil in her speech. But in the end she is bitter as a wormwood, Sharp as a two-edged sword. Her feet go to down to death, Her steps lay hold of Sheol. She does not ponder the path of life; Her ways are unstable, she does not know it.

Proverbs: 5:3–6

To sum up, let all be harmonious, sympathetic, brotherly, kindhearted, and humble in spirit; not returning evil for evil, or insult for insult, but giving a blessing instead; for you were called for that very purpose that you might inherit a blessing.

I Peter 3:8–9

The righteous cry and the Lord hears, And delivers them out of all their troubles. The Lord is near to the broken hearted, And saves those who are crushed in spirit.

Psalm 34:17–18

Questions

1. Has a stranger reached out to help you or guide you? If so, did you take their advice? As a stranger to someone else have you reached out to help someone?

2. Is it important to notice someone's actions/behavior before getting close to a person? List traits that bring up warning signs about a persons behavior?

3. When a person hurts you, how do you normally react?

4. What does it tell you about a person that does not fulfill a commitment or finish a project?

5. Why does it often take a tragic event for us to surrender our spirit to the Lord?

6. Too often in a relationship we allow someone to change our spirit to conform to their demands or expectations, which in many cases lead us to doubt or not like ourselves. Has this happened to you? How can we keep this from happening?

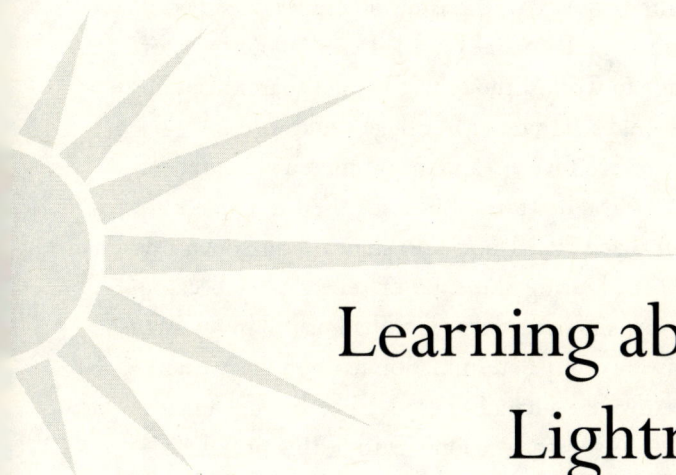

Learning about Lightness

During our separation, I became curious about Walt and why he offered to help us even though he did not know us. We were strangers to him. He was willing to sacrifice his precious time for us. I found out that Walt had a personal relationship with the Lord. He was a disciple for the Lord. He was living in lightness. I immediately bought a Bible to learn more. I started reading Proverbs and Ecclesiastes. For the first time in my life, the Bible made sense. I could understand it. I opened my heart to the word of God, and I found out about His forgiveness and His love. Once I understood the power of God, I knew Pam and I needed Him in our lives, individually and in our marriage. I realized without the Lord in our lives we only thought of ourselves the majority of the time. There was no special union in our lives. Pam and I needed God in our lives for our marriage to work. I thought if I could share this with Pam, she would see that our marriage could work.

Walt's concern for Pam and me prompted me to reflect on my life. I saw the times that Jesus tried to come into my life. I realized that I not did listen. I didn't open my heart to Him. During the time of reflection, I became aware of the many people that God had placed in my life. I became aware of my determination to do things without help from anyone—including God. I had not been ready to accept God's love or wisdom. During this time I realized when I was younger people tried to share the love of the Lord with me. I realized I was not ready during those times to accept His love and wisdom. Whatever the reason, until now I had never really opened my heart to the Lord. During this emotional time with Pam, I knew that I needed a spirit stronger than myself. I needed the Lord Jesus Christ to make it through this crisis in my life. I could not do it alone anymore.

> *For we know that if the earthly tent which is our house is torn down, we have a building from God, a house not made with hands, eternal in the heavens. For indeed in this house we groan, longing to be clothed with our dwelling from heaven;*
>
> II Corinthians 5:1–2

A few days after Pam left, she called me to tell me that she had told her dad that I had forced myself on her. I tried

to apologize to her for hurting her, but she did not want
to hear it. She said that her dad was really angry with me.
I asked if he knew all that had led up to that event and
if she told him all the facts of our life together. She did
not answer. I knew I had made a mistake, and she showed
me no mercy. She only thought about herself, not how
cruel she had been to me. She did not look at her own
actions and the hurt she brought to my heart. I told Pam
that I would go to her dad and apologize to him for hurting her. She made no comment. During the conversation
she demanded that if we were to get back together, then
I needed to see a counselor. She would require written
updates on my progress. I suggested that we both needed
help. After being separated I went to counseling a few
times, but she made no effort to get help.

> *For Judgment will be merciless to one who has shown
> no mercy; mercy triumphs over judgment.*
>
> James 2:13

I went to Charlie, her dad and told him what happened.
As a young man in my twenties, I was terrified, but knew I
loved this man and wanted him to know how I felt. With
God in his heart he said, "Son, I understand." He went on
to tell me of similar experiences in his own life. I never
wanted to hurt Pam or her dad. I loved them both. I did
talk to Charlie about the Lord at that time. I told him
that I had seen the changes in him. During our marriage,
I saw her dad change to a person that was more patient
and understanding with all people. I questioned at the

time how someone's spirit could change so dramatically. Because of my Bible study, I realized that he changed because of Jesus Christ. He shared some of his experiences he had with the Lord.

Charlie wanted Pam and me to go to Christian counseling, but Lucy, his wife, would not support him in the decision. Pam did not support my request for counseling. In the end, Pam said she did not love me any more and demanded a divorce. My worse fears were coming true. The person I loved most in this world was leaving me and going on in life without me. I knew in my heart that God could heal and repair our marriage the way it should be if both of us focused on the Lord. I prayed with all my heart for Pam to return to me, but she did not open her heart to Jesus Christ and our heavenly Father. She did not open her heart to me.

As I reflected on my time with Pam, I became curious about jealousy.[1] The definition, as I know it, is demanding complete devotion and being distrustfully watchful. What, I wonder, made my first wife a jealous person? If I returned a wave or offered one to someone I didn't know; she became incensed and accusing. Maybe it had something to do with her guilty conscience. I caution anyone to be very careful about entering into a relationship if that person exhibits jealousy. They can inhibit and suffocate you and perhaps be hiding a truth about themselves.

As I opened my heart to Jesus Christ and began reading the Bible, I started to find the answers to many of my questions about life, about people, and about myself. I had found out that love should be patient, kind and not jealous. I knew that I had joined the church at a young age, but now realized that I did not have the love of the Lord in my heart. My pledge to the church and to our Lord was insincere. I had no clue what the Bible really meant. I did not have the wisdom to ask for help or get counseling from a minister before we got married or during our marriage. It was too late for Pam and me when Walt arrived. My relationship with God was not strong enough to ask for and accept His wisdom earlier in my life even though I could feel His presence. Because the Lord was not the center of mine and Pam's life, the mistakes we made were magnified in the other's heart. We kept count of the good and bad deeds each of us did for and to each other. We did not have the love of Jesus Christ in our hearts, so it was difficult for us to truly forgive each other. I realized that our marriage was based on conditions. If I made Pam happy, she loved me; and if she was not happy, she would find someone that could make her feel happy, with little or no regard to the commitment of our marriage. Growing up with her family, she had learned that divorce was an acceptable solution; therefore, her commitment to our marriage was not very strong. If things did not go the way she wanted, Pam always knew there was a way out. I did not grow up with divorce, so I thought that when we married it would be forever. I had not understood that we needed the Lord in our marriage to make it work. Pam and I had started our lives together without His foundation. I was frantic to share this knowledge with Pam and wanted Him in our marriage for it to work. I was hoping for reconciliation in our marriage; Pam, however, was not interested in me or the Lord.

All Pam wanted now was her belongings that she
left behind before going away from me for good. She
didn't want to see me when she picked up her things; so
I arranged to be away from the apartment where I had
recently moved. This was very difficult for me because
I wanted to see her. While she was getting her belongings, she told the apartment manager that she was surprised I let the divorce happen so easily. I realized I could
not make Pam love me. Jesus showed me that love is a
decision. Jesus had been on my horizon all my life. He
was waiting for me to make the decision to love Him.
I decided to love Jesus for what He has done for me. It
boils down to a choice. Love is forever. As humans, we
may forget the exciting feelings that initially come with
falling in love; likewise, we may lose focus of how good
Jesus is to us. True love is forever, like Jesus. If I lose focus
on Jesus and stray, does He love me any less? The answer
is no. Jesus is the same all of the time. He forgives us and
His love is there for us even when we ignore Him.

I asked her dad before the divorce to ask Pam to meet
with me so we could talk. He told me that he had mentioned it to her, and she refused. She told him to stay out of
it. These are conditions she places on people since she does
not have the Lord in her heart. Things had to be solely her
way or no way. We should act more like Jesus and not use
our love in conditional ways. I would be in trouble if Jesus
used conditional love for me; when I do things that disap-
point Him, He would withdraw His love for me.

Pam found satisfaction in being single, and I found
satisfaction in finding Jesus Christ. The divorce shattered

my heart, but the Lord showed me so much about life. In the few short months before Pam asked for the divorce, I was never given the chance to share this with her. She seemed to be running from me, herself, maybe even from the Lord. Could she still be searching for the truth about life? Is she still treating people in the same manner she did when we were together? I pray that she has allowed Jesus Christ into her life. If searching for truth about life has been futile, the answers can be found in Jesus Christ.

Thoughts for Reflection

- It is never too late to accept the Lord into our lives unless we wait too long—until death. Hopefully right before our death we have one last opportunity to realize the love of the Lord and accept His grace. Don't wait too long; life can be over in a moment.

- Do not keep count of your brother's bad deeds, just as God does not keep count of ours.

- After I found God and started to depend on Him for His guidance, I still tried to do things my way. I made many mistakes. I still hurt people and myself with my actions and decisions. It takes years to mature spiritually and do it God's way.

- If we could all live by the *Golden Rule* which is to treat others as you would want to be treated, our lives would be more satisfying and the world would be a much better place.

Bible Verses for Study

"For I hate divorce," says the Lord, the God of Israel, "and him who covers his garment with wrong," says the Lord of hosts. "So take heed to your spirit, that you do not deal treacherously."

Malachi 2:16

And in that day you will ask Me no question. Truly, truly, I say to you, if you shall ask the Father for anything, He will give it to you in My name. Until now you have asked for nothing in My name: ask, and you will receive, that your joy may be made full.

John 16:23–24

Jesus said to them, I am the bread of life; he who comes to Me shall not hunger, and he who believes in Me shall never thirst.

John 6:35

And behold, they were bringing to Him a paralytic, lying on a bed; and Jesus seeing their faith said to the paralytic, "Take courage, My son, your sins are forgiven." And behold, some of the scribes said to themselves, "This fellow blasphemes." And Jesus knowing their thoughts said, "Why are you thinking even in your hearts? "For which is easier, to say, 'Your sins are forgiven,' or to say, 'Rise, and walk'? "But in order that you may know that the Son of Man has authority on earth to forgive sins"–then He said to the paralytic–"Rise, take up your bed, and go home."

Matthew 9:2–7

Questions

1. List the people involved in your life that you remember who have tried to share the joy of the Lord with you?

2. Each year or on a daily basis do you take time to reflect on your life and have the desire to make changes for the better? What changes would you make today?

3. Have you noticed a change in a person's life after they acknowledged accepting Jesus as his or her Savior? If so, what changes did you see in them?

4.   What is conditional love?

5.   Who gives us unconditional love?

6.   After we accept Christ, why are we considered a new creature?

7.   Why does God hate sin or even divorce?

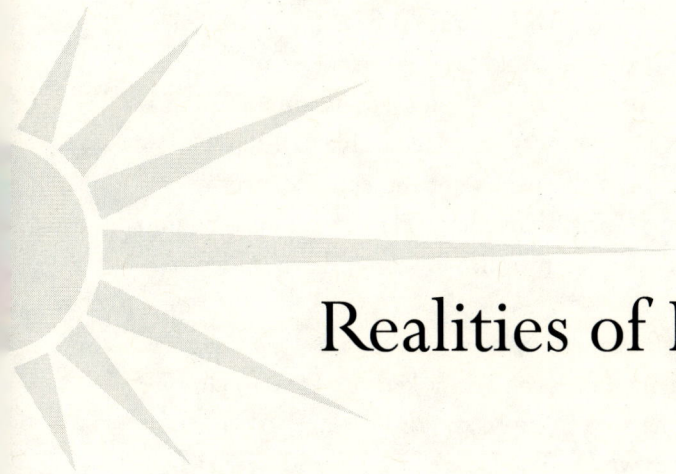

Realities of Life

Divorce was the cruelest event that had happened in my life. I was searching for answers. Why had I failed? Often, when we are at a low point in our lives, we carry guilt and place blame on ourselves; I carried both. Searching for the answer, I found God was not the center of our lives. The truth is I was not prepared for marriage because I did not have a personal relationship with the Lord. I was not the spiritual leader of our home. I was not even the spiritual leader of myself. Neither Pam nor I were focused on the Lord during our marriage or before our marriage. I had learned about God when I attended church as a child. I learned great Bible stories, the Ten Commandments, and about the love of Jesus. I did not take what I had learned and place it in my heart. It was only knowledge in my mind. I did not grow with the love of the Lord by placing what I learned in my heart. I did not have the wisdom to make the marriage work, nor did I have the communication skills that God could have given me. The Lord has made me a better communicator, and communication is vital in a relationship. We need to be able to listen. I know the divorce and the pain were the consequences of not having Jesus Christ in our lives. He did not lead me into that situation. I led myself. How often have we led ourselves into difficult situations?

During our marriage I begged Pam to stop lying and having affairs. Have you ever asked someone to change? She told me that a person couldn't change. I know now that she was wrong. The Lord's love can and does change the spirit of a person. I feel I have become a better person with Jesus Christ in my life. I am certainly glad that when I make mistakes the Lord does not say, "I do not love you any more, Mark." Based on my mistakes, I would receive very little love from Him. He forgives me for my mistakes when I ask Him. The hardest part for me is forgiving myself. Do you struggle with forgiving yourself? When I reflect on my first marriage, I believe that Pam was never faithful or committed to our relationship, yet I would not allow myself to see this before we got married. I was blinded by my love for her and could not see the truth about her. I had not looked at the whole person to whom I had given my heart. God can give us the insight to look at the whole person. I only wanted someone to love me. I did not realize that Jesus Christ has loved me since before I was born. I had not realized that the Lord had a better plan for my life if I let Him lead me. God gives us wisdom and knowledge while allowing us to have victory over sin through Jesus Christ.

> *Then the mystery was revealed to Daniel in a night vision. Then Daniel blessed the God of heaven; Daniel answered and said, "Let the name of God be blessed forever and ever, For wisdom and power belong to Him. "And it is He who changes the times and the epochs; He removes kings and establishes kings; He gives wisdom to wise men, And knowledge to men of understanding. It is He who reveals the profound and hidden things; He knows what is in the darkness, And the light dwells with Him.*
>
> Daniel 2:19–22

> *The sting of death is sin, and the power of sin is the law; but thanks be to God, who gives us the victory through our Lord Jesus Christ. Therefore, my beloved brethren, be steadfast, immovable, always abounding in the work of the Lord, knowing that your toil is not in vain in the Lord.*
>
> I Corinthians 15: 56–58

The light leads us to the knowledge that love should be patient, kind, and not jealous. I did not realize I was really searching for God's love. There is no love on earth like God's love. Even when we think we are happy and truly loved by another, we still feel something is missing in our lives. The missing link is the love of Jesus and the understanding of the sacrifice He made for us on the cross. God gave us the ultimate gift–His son Jesus. Jesus died on the cross so we have the free will to accept His love and have eternal life in heaven. We need the spiritual foundation in our lives to truly be happy. If you think you are in love, go to God for guidance and seek godly counsel in prayer. Listen to God in your heart. With God's help we can love someone forever by not keeping count of any wrongs. During this tough situation I realized a good example of worldly living is someone saying he or she does not love someone anymore. I feel they are justifying their actions by saying this. Unfortunately, in some cases a spouse still loves his or her mate, but cannot live with that person anymore because of abuse of some sort. God commands us not to put anything above Him, not even our spouses. He wants to fill the empty place in our soul with His love through Jesus Christ's love. God can change a person's heart and actions. Even with the Lord in our hearts, we often make the same mistakes over and over again until we come to a point in our lives we have had enough. Had I been willing to listen, I would not have gone through all the pain and hurt.

> *Love is patient, love is kind, and is not jealous; love does not brag and is not arrogant. Does not act unbecoming; it does not seek its own, is not provoked, does not take into account a wrong suffered, does not rejoice in unrighteousness, but rejoices with the truth; bears all things, believes all things, hopes all things and endures all things.*
>
> I Corinthians 13:4–7

Before my marriage, I thought I knew who I was. I believed that I was a moral person. I knew right from wrong. Since

I made the decision to have a personal relationship with the Lord, this relationship gives a whole new perspective to right and wrong. It is obvious Pam contributed to the destruction of our marriage through her lies and affairs, but I also contributed to the loss of our relationship. I put Pam before God. I became so confused and hurt from what was going on in our lives that I began to pull away from her. When I realized that I was losing her, I acted impulsively. I made a huge mistake after getting home from the bar. I know what I did was wrong. I have asked God for forgiveness. I know that God has forgiven me. In my meeting with Charlie, I told him I was sorry for my actions and I told Pam on the phone I was sorry for hurting her. Pam never allowed me to meet with her to ask for her forgiveness face to face. Always remember God will forgive us no matter what sin we have committed. Why do we have to repeat our mistakes over and over before we learn not to?

> *Like a dog that returns to its vomit is a fool who repeats his folly.*
>
> Proverbs 26:11

I now understand that "love as God intended" completes lives. Love should not destroy, love should not be demanding, and love should not be hurtful. Married people should complement each other. The Lord showed me that I was nothing without Him in my life. I know how cruel people can be without His love in their hearts. I know how hurtful I can be without his love in my heart. Do not forget: God feels everyone is special in His eyes because He created all of us in His image. With His love in my heart I am able to see all people in the way He does–with love and compassion.

Having Fun–Do Not Let Satan Steal Your Joy

I am thankful to Charlie for trying to get us Christian counseling. I understand Charlie was struggling in his own marriage, and he did not want to go against his wife's wishes. He had recently found the Lord, and Lucy did not have a personal relationship with the Lord. I knew it would be hard to keep this marriage together without Lucy's conversion to the Lord. I will reveal how their marriage turns out later. I understood that Charlie was a new Christian still unsure of the Lord's wishes. As a person grows with the Lord, I pray that he or she is able to become bold in Christ and stand up to his/her children and others.

Wise men store up knowledge, But with the mouth of the foolish, ruin is at hand.

Proverbs 10:14

As I was learning more about life and was awakened to the truth, I believe that many of our problems were amplified by Pam's background. Pam's mother left her father when their relationship got tough. Then her dad remarried, and his new wife was unfaithful. Pam saw the significant women in her life leaving or acting ungodly in the marriage relationship. So, Pam acted exactly as her role models. Many times events that occur in our lives affect our beliefs and our actions whether good or bad.

Thoughts for Reflection

- I now know that since I have a personal relationship with the Lord, I am never alone. I can always find support from the Bible and through prayer, even when no friends are around.

- Have the Lord's foundation in your life and home. If you try to found a relationship on your own, there is a good chance you are asking for failure. Statistics show that 50% of first marriages end in divorce. Are you willing to gamble with over a 50% chance of failure if you guide your own path?

- Depend on the Lord's wisdom. Let Him guide your life; otherwise, you will fall.

- The truth will set us free from turmoil. Living in the light is the way, the truth.

- God values each life and considers each as special. Once this concept is taken to heart, life becomes more meaningful, which gives us more confidence and purpose in life.

- We all make mistakes, and we always will because we are not Jesus. We must deal with our mistakes. Many times we make the same mistakes again and again until we learn to change paths. Ask God to make you a stronger and a better person. Most of all, ask His forgiveness. When you hurt someone, go to him or her and ask for forgiveness.

Bible Verses for Study

And why do you call Me, "Lord, Lord," and do not do what I say? Everyone who comes to Me, and hears My words, and acts upon them, I will show you whom he is like: he is like a man building a house, who dug deep and laid a foundation upon the rock; and when the flood rose, the torrent burst against that house and could not shake it, because it had been well built. But the one who has heard, and has not acted accordingly, is like a man who built a house upon the ground without any foundation; and the torrent burst against it and immediately it collapsed, and ruin of that house was great.

Luke 6:46–49

By wisdom a house is built, And by understanding it is established; And by knowledge the rooms are filled with precious and pleasant riches.

Proverbs 24:3–4

For if you are living according to the flesh, you must die; but if by the Spirit you are putting to death the deeds of the body, you will live.

Romans 8:13

If you keep My commandments, you will abide in My love; just as I have kept My Father's commandments, and abide in His love. These things I have spoken to you, that My joy may be in you, and that your joy may be made full.

John 15:10–11

Questions

1. Who is the spiritual leader of your family? Why is it important for a man to be the leader?

2. List ways you have led your own life and have failed?

3. Why is it important to have a spiritual foundation and listen to God's direction?

4. How does God complete your life?

5. Why is it hard for us to make a change in our lives?

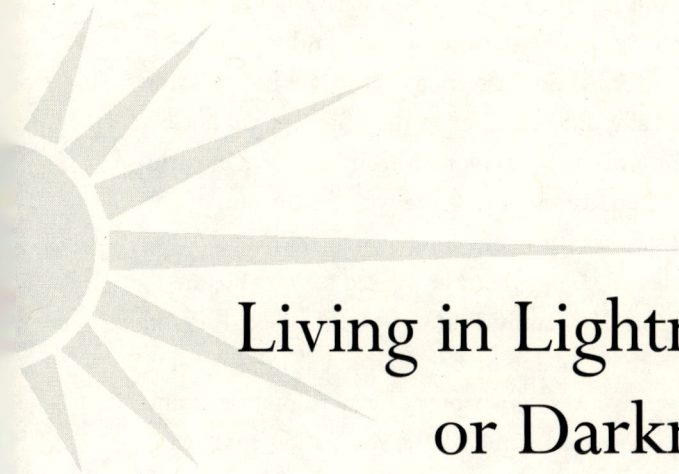

Living in Lightness
or Darkness

My heart was torn into many pieces. Have you ever felt sorry for yourself? I was deep into self-pity and wanted to die. I felt so alone. Why should I endure the pain when I could end the pain by dying? The pain of losing someone I loved almost as much as life itself was so great I thought I wanted to die. The divorce from Pam made me feel like I was a failure. I wallowed in my loss; at the time I was not looking ahead for the good things God had in store for me. I plotted several detailed ways to end my life. I thought about how my death would end the pain. I would not have to suffer any more. I wondered who would find my body and how long it would take to be found. I thought about how people that cared for me would feel. I thought about how Pam would react when she found out. Each time I was to the point of acting on the plot to kill myself, the Lord brought someone into my life to show me that I really did not want to die. One special person He brought into my life took me through a maze of paths and asked me questions along the way. At the end of the journey, I found the answer was not suicide. I realized that God had special things that He wanted for me. I came to the realization that Pam would not care if I died. She did not really care about me or our marriage. She was using our marriage as a safety net on her way to more exciting worldly adventures. I came to the realization that many people in the world had been in tougher situations than I. I should be thankful for my life. If I were to end my life, I would not get another chance at life. During this time I was in church trying to learn all I could about the Lord. The Lord was trying to lift me up to the light and Satan was trying to drag me down in darkness.

> *We must work the works of Him who sent ME, as long as it is day; night is coming, when no man can work. "While I am in the world, I am the light of the world.*
> John 9:4–5

At this point in my life, I could easily have turned to alcohol and/ or drugs to drown my sorrows. To some degree I did turn to alcohol, but not to the point of dependency. When I did drink, I consumed many drinks. Fortunately, I realized the danger ahead of me. The Lord did take the desire to drink away from me. I was amazed that when I tried to drink, I felt out of control and the desire to drink disappeared. That's what faith in the Lord is for. Alcohol and drugs are not an excuse to avoid dealing with difficult issues. Depend on the Lord and life will get better. At times I felt the Lord was actually carrying me when I was hurting so badly. If I can overcome and make my way with the Lord, anyone can.

Even though I had the Lord in my life, I still desperately wanted a partner in this life. I could not find a woman with whom to fall in love. I wanted to replace the void Pam left. I felt cold inside and not capable of loving again even though I wanted to love again. Before I could do that, I knew that I had to love myself again and take the time to heal. Less than a year later, I received a telephone call from Pam. My heart almost exploded with the anticipation of what she had to say. I hoped, irrationally, that she might say she had made a mistake and wanted to try again. Instead she said she had gotten a notice in the mail that we had made a mistake on our taxes a few years back. I told her to send the notice, gave her my address, and assured her I would take care of the matter. As soon as I asked her how she was, I knew I should have just said goodbye. Tauntingly, she said that she was remarried and was pregnant. I felt as though she was trying to hurt me even more. She was trying to hurt me. Obviously, I still had not moved on in my own life. All I could do at that point was to say that I hoped she was blessed with a good life and I hung up. I had to get off the phone because the tears were already in my eyes. I tried to end the conversation as Jesus would have, but the hurt was still there. Here I was miserable at losing her, and she is already remarried and expecting a child. Once again, I found myself wallowing in self-pity … wondering if she ever thought about the way she treated people, if she regretted lying to me and driving away our friends, if she knew that the comment about her being pregnant drove another stake into my heart, etc. I went outside and jumped into my Corvette to get away. My heart was in pain, and my response to the pain was to drive as fast as I could. At one point I went into a 360 degree spin and nearly hit a power pole. All I wanted to do was stop hurting. Since I was a new Christian, I didn't know that my faith in Christ would not alleviate all pain. But He was alongside of me. He walked with me and even carried me through the days that followed. Once, in the middle of crying, I suddenly realized I had almost made a terrible mistake. Killing myself wouldn't hurt Pam, and I would have missed out on the life in front of me. Was Satan reaching out to hurt me even more? Satan knew that I was still vulnerable to her.

Pam never sent the tax notice, which left me wondering why she had even called. The reason I am telling you this story is because I believe Jesus was with me in that Corvette. He saved my life. He told me to stop driving like an idiot.

It took me two years to see the light at the end of the tunnel. I cried often. I would wake up in the middle of the night in a sweat because of dreams. In my dreams, I would never be able to please Pam no matter what I did. I felt that God was speaking to me, letting me know that the relationship would never have worked. She was not a happy person, and nothing I could do would ever change that. Jesus could change her if she would open her heart to Him. I realized until she chose Jesus' path she would continue to search for happiness. Over the years, with God's love, the pain has lessened, but it is still part of me. Every time I hear about someone getting divorced, it penetrates my heart. I know the pain. God knows the pain His children are going through and it makes Him hurt. He loves us. I still think about Pam. I wonder if she will have to lose someone dear to her one day in order to find the love of Jesus. Often it takes losing something we place before God to wake us. How many more people will she hurt along her way in life? What kind of morals and values is she teaching her children by her actions? I prayed for her redemption.

Soon, I began to depend on the Lord more, and I ultimately found myself in a relationship with Him. It brought a peace to my life that I never thought possible. I prayed for Him to send me my life's mate. I continued my relationship with Walt and became involved in his church. As a new child in Christ, I was surprised at the turmoil there. Once I became involved in the church, I realized why God had written that many people in church will not make it to heaven. Many of them were doing Satan's work. Walt was trying hard to do the Lord's work, but there was a large group of members trying to split the church. One of the main leaders trying to cause havoc in the church was Roger.

It was apparent Roger physically abused his wife since

she wasn't always able to hide the bruises. She would wear dark sunglasses to church to hide her black eyes. It became so bad that she called Walt and the deacons of the church to ask for help. This was the right thing to do. She knew that God would want her to do everything she could to save her marriage. A few days after the churchmen visited Roger's home, Roger became convinced that everyone knew what was going on in his private life. He was sure Walt was spreading the gossip and began to talk to people in town to refute what he thought they already knew. Walt had not said anything to anybody. However, Roger's own guilty conscience did spread the news. Roger came to me, and asked if Walt told me the details about the night his wife called the deacons to his house. He also requested that I side with him in this matter. I politely refused to side with him. As I watched Roger, I realized that he used Jesus and the church to boast about his own accomplishments. He was always talking about how many people he had brought to Christ and how he had done this or that. He made no mention of the Lord when he spoke. During that time many church members treated Walt's wife and children very badly and they ended up leaving my church. Roger and others succeeded in splitting the church. Once Walt was gone, Roger and individuals that sided with him to split the church left our church and started to form another church in town.

Eventually, Roger's wife divorced him. His children had very little to do with their father. It is not God's will to see families destroyed. Jesus could have changed his life for the better before he lost his family. Jesus was close to

Roger by working through Walt. It is important to look at the direction our lives are going. We may need to stop and ask the Lord to help us make a change in our lives. Is this path of life bringing happiness to you? Did Roger only have the Lord in his mind and not in his heart?

I wanted to share this about Roger, a person causing the split in the church; often we profess to know the Lord while our actions show others God is not the center of our lives. It is all about us. I personally professed to know the Lord at a young age, but did not have a clue about His love and forgiveness. When I realized what Jesus Christ did for me on the cross, my life changed. It was a spiritual awakening for me. I could feel the pain He suffered for me on the cross, yet at the same time, I felt in my heart His love. I realized I should not place my focus on myself, but my focus should be on others.

> Furthermore, I have seen under the sun that in the place of justice there is wickedness, and in the place of righteousness there is wickedness.
>
> Ecclesiastes 3:16

> And He was passing through from one city and village to another, teaching, and proceeding on His way to Jerusalem. And someone said to Him, "Lord, are there just a few who are being saved?" And he said to them, "Strive to enter by the narrow door; for many, I tell you, will seek to enter and will not be able. "Once the head of the house gets up and shuts the door, and you begin to stand outside and knock on the door, saying 'Lord, open up to us!' then He will answer and say to

you, 'I do not know where you are from.' Then you will
begin to say, 'We ate and drank in Your presence, and
You taught our streets'; and He will say, 'I tell you, I
do not know where you are from; DEPART FROM
ME, ALL EVILDOERS.'

Luke 13:22–27

During the years I spent alone after my divorce, I realized that I was the only one who could take blame for my decisions. With God at my side, I started taking responsibility for myself, including the mistakes I made. Too often it is easy to blame others for our mistakes. Finding the Lord has helped me to see that I made many mistakes in my marriage to Pam. As a single person I made mistakes everyday. We will all have to account for our deeds at the gates of heaven if we do not face our mistakes here on earth. Our choices are to go through life blaming someone or something else or make a commitment to act according to God's laws. We can decide to carry love or hate in our hearts; I know that God does not want us to hate someone. I would be the one to suffer if I had hate in my heart. My spirit would be destroyed, and my soul would be in limbo. Blaming others is only an excuse for our mistakes. Do not live your life full of excuses and "what if's." In the end, you will only live a regretful life! I have often had regrets but have tried to learn from my mistakes.

I am thankful that God does not stop loving us even when we are not in His will. He forgives and continues to forgive through His Son, even as I continue to make mistakes. I pray that you will allow Jesus Christ to come into your life before you miss the opportunity to find the love of our Lord. Praying for others, even those we don't respect, softens our hearts. God has softened my heart toward Pam because I continue to pray for her.

I realize we are all created by God. We are meant to use the gifts He gave us for His Glory, not our glory. Each one of us is special in His eyes. I can see clearer now having this knowledge.

> *But I say to you who hear, love your enemies, do good to those who hate you, bless those who curse you, pray for those who mistreat you.*
>
> Luke 6:27

> *Do not be eager in your heart to be angry, For anger resides in the bosom of fools.*
>
> Ecclesiastes 7:9

One thing that happened after my divorce was that I became acutely aware of other people's relationships. It was disappointing to see how many people were looking outside their marriages for happiness, not only men looking for other women but men looking for love with men. It surprised me when a friend with whom I worked tried this path. I asked him about his lifestyle, and he said that he was born that way. I decided to share God's word on homosexuality with him. I copied Bible scriptures pertaining to this issue onto index cards and gave them to him. I tried to explain that based on what God says, his lifestyle was wrong, and I suggested that he ask God for guidance. His response was that I sounded like his mom. He told me bluntly that if he wanted to, he could manipulate me and draw me into his world. I knew in my heart that homosexuality was not a struggle that God was using in my life, so I told my friend that it would be a waste of his energy. I shared God's words with him in a non-judgmental manner, not condemning him, just his actions. I heard from him eight years later and his lifestyle was the same. I continue to pray for him and his personal struggle just as Jesus Christ would have me do.

> *and immoral men and homosexuals and kidnappers and liars and perjurers, and whatever else is contrary to sound teaching, according to the glorious gospel of the blessed God, with which I have been entrusted.*
>
> I Timothy 1:10

> *You shall not lie with a male as one lies with a female; it is abomination.*
>
> Leviticus 18:22

> *If there is a man who lies with a male as those who lie with a woman, both of them have committed a detestable act; they shall surely be put to death. Their bloodguiltiness is upon them.*
>
> Leviticus 20:13

During the time that I was single, I longed for a life mate. I was lonely and wanted to share my life with someone. I still wanted to have a child. I dated but did not find anyone that held the Lord in her heart. God kept telling me to wait for the right one. I did find Becky, a beautiful lady that loved the Lord, but she was not ready for a serious relationship because she had recently gone through a divorce. She and her young son were heart broken by the breakup of their home. Becky's husband was expecting another child with someone else and had decided to divorce Becky in order to marry the other woman. It will be interesting to see if that marriage will be honored by either one of them. Will Becky's ex-husband destroy his second marriage, leaving yet another devastated wife and child? What kind of behavior does this teach the children? I believe God does not want or like divorces because of the hurt and disruption it causes in lives.

To occupy my time I began playing church-league softball as well as meeting new friends. I broke my ankle severely playing ball. The break required surgery. I was all alone in a town where I did not have family. I was amazed when the Stancill family who did not know me very well offered to take me in and help me during this difficult time. I accepted their generous offer. They acted as though I was a member of their family. They waited on me hand and foot since I could not get around at all for weeks. I enjoyed their young children coming to my room to spend time with me. It was a blessing to hug and to play with their tiny daughter. She was precious. This gave me hope that I could have a family of my own one day and share my life. The Stancills were living their lives for the Lord and helping people when they could. During this time their love for me reinforced what God is about.

After my relationship with Becky, I continued to struggle with dating. Becky was a very special person; her rejection hurt me deeply. I continued to search for someone to love me. I allowed one particular woman to get too close to me even though I knew I did not want to marry her. I told her that we would not get married, yet I allowed an intimate relationship to develop. Upon reflection, I realized that my actions with this woman were not that different from Becky's husband's actions with the other woman. Both of us were looking for love outside of God's laws. Just as Becky's husband's actions hurt her, just as Pam hurt me, I had hurt this lady. If we follow God's instructions, a lot of pain could have been avoided. At this point I had God in my heart, but I did not have the faith that could enable me to completely turn my life over to Him.

With God in my heart I understood how so many people were truly missing God's plan for them. There were so many people confused and hurt. Yet amid all the confusion, I saw people like Walt trying to carry on life with the Lord at the center of his life. In my new church I became friends with David and Susan. They lived their lives with the Lord at the center of their personal and family lives. Through watching David and Susan, I could see that the Lord's way was the only way for a marriage to be successful.

After moving away from the community where I met David and Susan, I lost contact with them. Years later David tracked me down. It was such a blessing to fellowship with him and his family again. The reconnection to these godly people affirmed for me that people trying to grow in the Lord and do His work can have a lasting relationship and marriage.

I realized that walking with Jesus was tough because I had to relinquish my personal life to God and give up my worldly desires. I had to believe that God knows and wants what is best for me. The temptations of not living in His word were great. I realized then and still acknowledge that following God's will for my life is hard, and I often fall short.

Thoughts for Reflection

- I believe God knows and wants the best for me. I must stay focused on Him in order to achieve what is best.

- Often I realize things I need to change about myself that would make me become a better person. It is frustrating that I can not immediately make a change for the better. I sometimes think change does not come quickly in my life, so I depend on God more.

- Having a personal relationship with the Lord meant I had to live by His rules not mine. Often I found myself with selfish desires that I only could justify as being right. Once I carried out the wrongful desires, my heart would be penetrated with the truth that I was wrong. My failure did not bring joy to my heart. My failure only brings sadness.

- After my divorce I was trying to figure out about life. I hurt a few people because of my selfish desires–if I had only listened to the Lord instead of living for the moment.

- If life seems hopeless and you find yourself contemplating suicide, ask God for His guidance. He will show you that life is worth living in spite of your present circumstance. He will show you that you are a special person no matter what someone has said or the way life has treated you.

- It is easy after a breakup of a marriage or with a girl/boy friend to feel like you can never love someone again. Holding onto anger, guilt, and resentment hurts us more. It hurts when we are rejected. We become overly cautious. With the Lord in our lives, this doubt can be overcome. We can love again with the Lord in our hearts. Trust only in His guidance.

Bible Verses for Study

Indeed, there is not a righteous man on earth who continually does good and who never sins.

Ecclesiastes 7:20

"But from the beginning of creation, God Made Them Male and Female. "For this cause a man shall leave his father and mother, "And the two shall become one flesh; consequently they are no longer two, but one flesh. What therefore God has joined together let no man separate.

Mark 10:6–9

Therefore I say to you, all things for which you pray and ask, believe that you have received them, and they shall be granted you.

Mark 11:24

Hate evil, you who love the Lord, Who preserves the soul of His godly ones; He delivers them from the hand of the wicked.

Psalm 97:10

Teach me to do Thy will, For Thou art my God; Let Thy good Spirit lead me on level ground.

Psalm 143:10

Questions

1. How can God mend a broken relationship?

2. Does God always answer your prayers the way you want?

3. Has God ever spoken to you through your dreams?

4. How can we stop hurting ourselves or someone else?

5. Why does rejection by someone loving us often hurt so much?

6. Why is it important to pray?

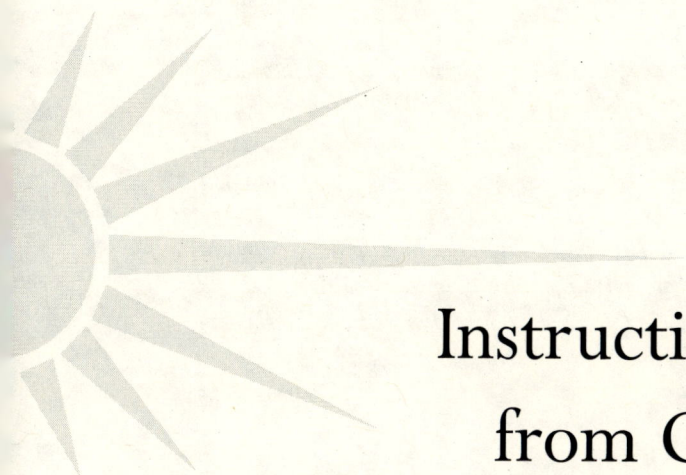

Instructions from God

The Bible is a book written about God, Jesus, and people. Many of the scenarios are about trials, tribulations, faith, and the way we should live our lives. There are many parables in the Bible. A parable is a simple story told to illustrate a godly truth. The Bible shows us that when we live His way, we are blessed. It is a book of wisdom, and it gives us guidance in the way that we should live. If we do not focus on God, then there are consequences to face. These are often either hurtful to ourselves or to others. The Bible alone answers the greatest questions we face during our lives: *"Why am I here on earth?" "How can I know the truth about life?" "What happens after I die?"*

In the beginning God created the heavens and the earth.

Genesis 1:1

But now, thus says the Lord, your Creator, O Jacob, And He who informed you, O Israel, "Do not fear, for I have redeemed you; I have called you by name; you are Mine!

Isaiah 43:1

"Far be it from Thee to do such a thing, to slay the righteous with the wicked, so that the righteous and the wicked are treated alike. Far be from Thee! Shall not the Judge of all earth deal justly?

Genesis 18:25

Below I have listed the Laws of God. Many of you have learned or heard about them either in church or Sunday school or from family and friends. Please, take a moment and really hear what the words are saying.

Then the Lord said to Moses, "Write down these words, for accordance with these words I have made a covenant with you and Israel." So he was there with the Lord forty days and forty nights; he did not eat bread or drink water. And he wrote on the tablets the words of the covenant, The Ten Commandments.

Exodus 34:27–28

For of His fullness we have all received, and grace upon grace. For the Law was given through Moses; grace and truth were realized through Jesus Christ. No man has seen God at any time; the only begotten God, who is in the bosom of the Father, He has explained Him.

John 1:16–18

The 10 Commandments

Then God spoke all these words, saying, I am the Lord your God, who brought you out of the land of Egypt, out of the house of slavery. [1ˢᵗ] You shall have no other gods before Me. [2ⁿᵈ] You shall not make for yourself an idol, or any likeness of what of what is in heaven above or on earth beneath or the water under the earth. You shall not worship them or serve them; for I, the Lord your God, am a jealous God, visiting the iniquity of the fathers on the children on the third and the fourth generations of those who hate Me, but showing loving kindness to thousands, to those who love Me and keep My commandments. [3ʳᵈ] You shall not take the name of the Lord in vain, for the Lord will not leave him unpunished who takes His name in vain. [4ᵗʰ] Remember the Sabbath day, to keep it holy. Six days you shall labor and do all your work, but the seventh day is a Sabbath of the Lord your God; in it you shall not do any work, you or your son or your daughter, your male or your female servant or your cattle or your sojourner who stays with you. For in six days the Lord made the heavens and the earth, the sea and all that is in them, and rested on the seventh day; therefore the Lord blessed the Sabbath day and made it holy. [5ᵗʰ] Honor your father and your mother, that your days may be prolonged in the land which the Lord your God gives you. [6ᵗʰ] You shall not murder. [7ᵗʰ] You shall not commit adultery. [8ᵗʰ] You shall not steal. [9ᵗʰ] You shall not bear false witness against your neighbor. [10ᵗʰ] You shall not covet your neighbor's house; you shall not covet your neighbor's wife or his male servant or his female servant or his ox or his donkey or anything that belongs to your neighbor.

Exodus 20:1–17

> *The conclusion, when all has been heard, is: fear God*
> *and keep His commandments, because this applies to*
> *every person. For God will bring every act to judgment,*
> *everything which is hidden whether it is good or evil.*
>
> Ecclesiastes 12:13–14

Upon reflection, you may notice that a few man-made laws are similar to God's laws. God gave His people the Ten Commandments as principles which embrace the whole order of life in relationships so we can live safely and in peace with Him and one another. My wish is that everyone has the Lord in his or her life and heart.

I realized that once I found God it was hard to live up to His commandments. In some ways I fell short of His commandments; daily, I would sin. Realization set in that I could never be perfect like Jesus. Even though I could not become perfect did not mean I should ignore all of His commandments and still expect my reward to be heaven. I still needed to have my sights on Jesus daily while striving to become more like Him. I needed to carry God's spirit in my life daily–God's love. To keep His spirit in my life, I needed to follow God's word; I needed to learn more about what was written in the Bible. Since I always fell short of His commandments, I learned to appreciate God's mercy and grace, and all the more, His forgiveness. God in the verses below, states it clearly that we cannot be perfect:

> *Even the righteousness of God through faith in Jesus*
> *Christ for all those who believe; for there is no distinction;*
> *for all have sinned and fall short of the glory of God.*
>
> Romans 3:21–23

As children of God, we are meant to live focusing on Jesus and His ways, not on selfish gains. We need to focus on what Jesus did for us on the cross. When we do this, we get the most out of life. We should share our love, be forgiving, and do for others as God would have us do. When doing these good things we are in turn rewarded with more than we can ever imagine. Sometimes our actions may impact a person in such a way that he or she wants to know why we are the way we are. We need to stop focusing on what someone can do for us and ask ourselves what we can do for others. If we are boastful and keep count of our good deeds, which is prideful, we will not be rewarded in heaven.

When I opened my heart to the Lord, He spoke to me through my conscience. If I stop and listen to the Lord, He tells me what is right and wrong. God is faithful. He will lead us in the direction that is best for us if we take the time to allow our *souls* to hear Him. All too often we are hurried, stressed, panicked, or blinded by the passion of the moment, and we don't take the time to breathe and center ourselves so we can listen. Without His guidance and a commitment to His basic commandments, there is chaos. Imagine a world without war, murder, hatred, greed, screaming at each other, cutting each other down, making fun of others, blaming others for our mistakes or misfortunes, etc. We may not be able to change the whole world in our lifetime, but we can start by changing ourselves and the world around us.

To begin, we need to show the love of Jesus at home. We cannot expect our children to understand the love of Jesus simply by taking them to church. We must teach them at home through God's word and by example. We must start when they are very small and teach at their level. Imagine what the world would be like if all of us tried to treat others the way Jesus would treat us. I know that it starts with me and that my life is so much better for my acceptance of His way. Is it really human nature to bring pain to others, even those we love? We can repent to God and ask the person for forgiveness, but although our anger may dissipate, the hurt inflicted may not. For many of us, it is difficult to ask for forgiveness. Jesus can help us find the place within ourselves to make that possible. Based on my own experience, I believe that many of us have not taken the time to reflect about life and come to the realization that God's path is the way to go. It took me failing in my first marriage before I realized I needed spiritual help; I was broken. When I made the decision to feel God's love, a deeper appreciation for my life and the people involved in it grew inside me.

> *Do not call to mind the former things, Or ponder things of the past. "Behold I will do something new, Now it will spring forth; Will you not be aware of it? I will even make a roadway in the wilderness, rivers in the desert.*
>
> Isaiah 43:18–19

I realized I needed to incorporate what I learned in Sunday school and church into my life. The key is I needed to be in attendance so I could learn more and better understand. Ministers and many Sunday school teachers have so much knowledge to share about the Bible; they can be excellent teachers if we decide to listen and learn. In order to take the lessons of Sunday school, church and the Bible into my heart, I had to understand the sacrifice that Jesus made for me on the cross. Only then would I be able to fully understand Jesus' pain and what He accomplished during His time on earth. When I allowed my spirit to accept Jesus Christ as my Lord and Savior during my own personal crisis, I could also allow Him to mend my broken heart. Through this acceptance I began to understand life and the way I should live. I hope that my story will in some way encourage you to seek a personal relationship with Jesus Christ before you experience any overwhelming pain as I did. I sometimes wonder why I did not accept Christ's love when I was younger; especially that stormy night that He appeared to me. When you have finished the story, I hope your questions about life will be answered.

Thoughts for Reflection

- Life is good. Life is the best knowing Jesus.

- When I "get down" on life and myself, I often think of others that have it much tougher. I then give thanks to God for this time of my life.

- Depend on the Lord during the tough times. Your faith will strengthen.

- Have you noticed how sometimes people disappear from your life even when you think of them as a friend. I often wonder why they crossed my path. I sometimes think God wonders about me when I disappear and don't depend on Him daily.

- Ask God for direction in your life, and He will lead you.

- If we listen, we can learn. If we open our hearts to the Lord, we can change.

- The Bible is God's instructions and guidance for us. Through studying the Bible, God's words produce change in us. The change makes our faith stronger during adverse times, builds character, infuses hope, gives us understanding about life and guarantees our future in eternity. We must take His teachings and apply them to our lives. Life on earth is not perfect because we will never be perfect. We can have an abundant, joyful and peaceful life if we depend on God. Perfection will be heaven.

Bible Verses for Study

For the word of God is living and active and sharper than a two-edged sword, and piercing as far as the division of soul and spirit, of both joints and marrow, and able to judge the thoughts and intentions of the heart.

Hebrews 4:12

I said to myself, "God will judge both the righteous man and the wicked man, for a time for every matter and for every deed is there.

Ecclesiastes 3:17

Teacher, which is the great commandment in the Law? And He said to him, "You shall love the

Lord your God with all your heart, and with all your soul, and with all your mind." This is the great and foremost commandment. The second is like it, "You shall love your neighbor as yourself." On these two commandments depend the whole Law and the Prophets.

Matthew 22:36–40

All Scripture is inspired by God and profitable for teaching, for reproof, for correction, for training in righteous.

II Timothy 3:16

If you love Me, you will keep My commandments.

John 14:15

The tongue of the righteous is as choice silver, The heart of the wicked is worth little. The lips of the righteous feed many, But fools die for lack of understanding. It is the blessing of the Lord that makes rich, and He adds no sorrow to it.

Proverbs 10:20–22

Or do you think that the Scripture speaks to no purpose: "He jealously desires the Spirit which He has made to dwell in us"? But He gives a greater grace, Therefore it says, "God is opposed to the proud, but gives grace to the humble. "Submit therefore to God. Resist the devil and he will flee from you.

James 4:5–7

Questions

1. Why is it important to be involved in Sunday school and church?

2. What ways can you strengthen your spiritual faith?

3. How do you know when the Lord is trying to direct you?

4. Why is it important to live by the two greatest commandments mentioned in Matthew 22:36–40?

God at the Center

After my divorce, I remained single for almost nine years. After having my heart shattered during my first marriage, I was hesitant to give my heart to just anyone. Often people never recover from a broken heart and are not willing to place themselves in a relationship to be hurt again. I was waiting on God to show me who was the right person to marry. I realized that it (the marriage) had been the focus rather than my relationship with God. I began to think I was getting too old to find that special person. I almost accepted I would be a bachelor without the joy of having a family for the rest of my life. I felt alone in the world even though I carried God in my heart. When I returned to my parent's home to visit, the void left by not having a wife and children was magnified. During one of these visits

I decided to visit Joyce, whose children with whom I had grown up. While I was there, I asked how her children were doing. Her son Jamey and I played football on the same high school football team. I dated her oldest daughter Kelly a few times in high school. Her youngest daughter Letha and I were friends even in college. I found out that Kelly was single at the time, so I asked for her address.

Something in my heart told me that I should write her. I wanted to find out if she had the Lord in her life, since Joyce told me she was experiencing a painful time. I wanted to give her some notice before I called her, so I thought a letter would be the best way to communicate with her initially. I wrote about what the Lord was trying to do in my life, and I hoped that He was part of her life, too. I gave it a few weeks before I called her. I was very nervous for some reason. During our conversation Kelly said that her family was planning a Thanksgiving feast at her mom's house in our hometown. We planned to visit with each other over the Thanksgiving holidays. After our visit we began dating. I could see the dedication of her heart to the Lord. She was more dedicated than I was. He was the center of her life. I felt confident that this was the lady God wanted me to be with after so many years of asking God for a life mate. We spent many hours together just talking and holding each other. Being with Kelly felt right. She was a beautiful person outside and inside since she loved the Lord. Her actions showed me that her heart was focused on the Lord. I made a decision to give her my heart, and she accepted my marriage proposal.

How blessed is the man who finds wisdom, And the man who gains understanding. For its profit is better than the profit of silver, And its gain than gold. She is more precious than jewels; And nothing you desire compares with her.

Proverbs 3:13–15

After we announced our engagement, my dad told us that if we wanted him to be at our wedding, we needed to get married soon because he would not be around much longer. We moved the wedding date up. Two months after our wedding, my dad passed away. I know my dad is in heaven. My sister was in the room right before he went home to Jesus. She said my dad raised his frail body up from the bed and reached out saying, "Jesus, I'm coming home." Jesus came to bring him home.

My mother was really struggling with her health and the sadness of losing dad. She shared with my sister and me that she did not want to spend Christmas without my dad. She went to be with Jesus and her husband the day before Christmas Eve. One of the hardest things to accept concerning their deaths was they never got to see their grandson, my little boy. A few weeks after mom's death, Kelly and I found out we were going to have a child. The sadness over my parents never seeing my son is eased by the blessing that I know I will get to see them again in heaven one day, and so will my son. Before their deaths, the Lord answered one of my mother's most adamant prayers. She was deeply concerned that I did not have Jesus in my heart. She lived to see me suffer through my divorce and the resulting change in my heart as I opened up to the

Lord. During the time after my divorce, I became closer to my parents. With the Lord's help, I was able to understand and forgive issues that had kept us distant.

Everything seemed good in the beginning of our marriage, but Kelly knew something was not right. I had a major problem. Loving her meant I had to give my heart to her totally. Satan was telling me to have fear and discontentment in my marriage. She knew I was not giving myself totally to her. The emotional and physical intimacy was missing. We became more like two people living in the same house, not one together. My heart had been terribly damaged in my first marriage, so I began building walls to keep from getting hurt again. Satan was pleased with my withdrawal. I wanted to have a godly marriage, but deep down I was still hurting from my first marriage. I had not gotten over the betrayal I had experienced. The scars and wounds went beyond my heart and into my soul. When Kelly got impatient with me and lost her temper, I simply placed the walls higher. After several years she realized that she would not be able to change me through talking, screaming or any other human action.

While we were dating, I had shown Kelly the person I wanted to be, a caring person that loved the Lord. She fell in love with that person, not the person that kept pulling away and building walls. My actions confused and frustrated her, yet she never lost sight of the person she fell in love with. Instead of destroying me with cruel comments and unfaithfulness, she went to God for answers. She began to pray for me and our marriage. She tried to see me through God's eyes. It was not easy for her to give up control of our marriage. But she had tried everything. She knew our only hope was God.

The wise woman builds her house, but the foolish tears it down with her own hands.

Proverbs 14:1

I was afraid to tell her my heart was still broken from the hurt I experienced in my first marriage. I was scared to totally give my heart to her. I had given someone my heart before and look what happened. The bottom line is that I should have gone to her and told her my feelings. Our marriage would have gotten better sooner if I had been open with her. I was not focusing on God each day in my life and did not realize the blessing He had given me. I let my past relationship hurt our marriage. Finally, with God's help, I went to her and told her about my fears. Kelly did not make fun or cut me down like Pam would have. She showed me compassion and love. I eventually apologized to her for hurting her. God showed me that Kelly's love is a true blessing. God showed me His way is the only way. During the writing of this story, God has moved me to thank Kelly for loving me. Have you thanked someone lately for being in your life?

With the Lord's love in her heart, Kelly draws people into her life instead of running them off. She is building our home with the Lord at the center, not tearing it down by keeping count of my wrongs. She does not tear our home down with human weaknesses; instead, she depends on the Lord for patience. I am blessed through her faith.

If Kelly had not turned to the Lord, my second home would have washed away in the sand just as my first home. Her love for the Lord has brought us a good marriage and many friends. She has a solid foundation in the Lord.

I shared with Kelly that many years ago God had placed the desire in my heart to write a story about my struggles in life. I also told her that the desire to write the story had recently returned. I believe God wanted me to experience Kelly's godly love along with the love of my son before I could share my story with others. God has given me more than I ever could have asked for.

> *Bless the Lord, O my soul, And forget none of His benefits; Who pardons all your iniquities; Who heals all your diseases; Who redeems your life from the pit; Who crowns you with loving kindness and compassion; Who satisfies your years with good things, So that your youth is renewed like the eagle.*
>
> Psalm 103:2–5

Kelly has been very supportive even though I have doubted myself during the writing of this story. I doubted my ability to write a book because writing was not one of my passions in school. My passion was sports. I wondered why anyone would want to hear my story, but she encouraged me to write. She said I should finish the story and let God lead me. I agreed. I realized if I did not listen to my heart, I could miss out on another blessing my Lord has in store for me. I have prayed each day for the Lord to show me what he wants me to share in this story. Reliving the experience of my first marriage has been painful. I told Kelly one day I was traveling on the interstate thinking about what went on in my first marriage when I realized I had tears rolling down my cheeks. She gave me a hug and held me. What a change from the turmoil of my first marriage! Do you like to have turmoil in your life? Over the years, my love for my wife has grown stronger with the Lord in our lives. With the Lord in our hearts and marriage, I know we will be blessed, and that He will walk with us through the hard times and good times.

When we marry, the union should complement and make the other person better. I have to say Kelly has helped me become a better person and I am blessed to have her in my life. With her suggestions, ideas, insight and love for the Lord, the book has become much better. She is a spectacular mom and a beautiful wife. My son and I are blessed to have her in our lives.

Thoughts for Reflection

- The Lord brings us many benefits such as peace, joy, knowledge, salvation, grace, love and especially a solid foundation to build our lives together.

- Do not forget why you fell in love with your life partner. Stay faithful to that person. Cherish the good times. Work through the tough times together.

- Work on family issues with each other to keep the family together.

- When your spouse or loved one asks you a question and you do not know how to respond, consider saying, "Let's see what the Bible has to say about that."

- Life is about building relationships with God as our foundation.

Bible Verses for Study

Nevertheless let each individual among you also love his own wife even as himself; and let the wife see to it that she respect her husband.

Ephesians 5:33

Enjoy life with the woman whom you love all the days of your fleeting life which He has given to you under the sun; for this is your reward in life, and in your toil in which you have labored under the sun.

Ecclesiastes 9:7

Husbands, love your wives, just as Christ also loved the church and gave Himself up for her;

Ephesians 5:25

Let the husband fulfill his duty to his wife, and likewise also the wife to her husband. The wife does not have authority over her own body, but the husband does; and likewise also the husband does not have authority over his own body, but the wife does. Stop depriving one another for a time that you may devote yourselves to prayer, and come together again lest Satan tempt you because of your lack of self control.

I Corinthians7:3–5

Let your fountain be blessed, And rejoice in the wife of your youth, As a loving hind and graceful doe, Let her breasts satisfy you at all times; Be exhilarated always with her love.

Proverbs: 5:18–20

Questions

1. Why do many of us have to suffer through a mistake or hurt in order to realize and find the love of Jesus Christ?

2. What is your perception of love? How should it be?

3. How does a wise woman build her home?

4. List any blessing that you may have missed out on or more you could have accomplished because you did not follow our Lord's direction.

5. Why do we too often let down or hurt the people we love and care about the most?

Life Foundations

There are three foundations on which your life and home can be built. It can be built on a Foundation of Rock, because both people in the marriage love the Lord, a Foundation of Clay, where one person loves the Lord and the other does not, or a Foundation of Sand, in which neither person has the Lord in his or her life. My first marriage was built on a foundation of sand. Upon which foundation is your home and your life built.

Foundation of Rock

If you are about to get married or you are married, the best choice is to live as one with God's love in both of your hearts. If you do, the chance of your marriage lasting is very good. You must work to stay focused on the Lord. You may ask why so many

Christian marriages end in divorce. Just because we say we are a Christian and believe in God does not mean we have a personal relationship with Him or that our lives are perfect; we all make mistakes. I claimed to be a Christian when I joined the church at a young age, but I had no idea what the Lord meant in my heart. I only knew Him intellectually, not spiritually. When I accepted Jesus Christ as my Savior, I could feel His pain of dying on the cross for me since I was in pain myself. When I felt His pain, He touched my heart. Many people proclaim to be Christians, but are what they proclaim based on a worldly values system.

Foundation of Clay

If one spouse loves the Lord and the other does not, the marriage will have difficult times. Although the person with the Lord in his or her heart will be praying for the one he or she loves, one may not be able to change his or her mate. Should a person stay in an abusive marriage whether it is mental or physical abuse or both while trying to bring his or her spouse to the Lord? I can only suggest praying seriously for the answer. The Lord will give you peace about your decision. In some cases the nonbeliever will ask for a divorce or be comfortable living a dual life. When I say "dual life" this is the situation in which someone wants to have the image of having a Christian marriage and family, but they are too selfish thinking only about themselves while living a worldly life. This is confusing, but it happens. The person is only concerned about his or her happiness, not the family's happiness.

Foundation of Sand

When people do not have the Lord in their lives, the marriage is less likely to last. There is a tendency to keep score of the good things and bad things we do for and to each other. Issues become magnified. Conflicts arise, and there is no guidance for ways to solve them. In time it may be too late for a solution, and the marriage is over. My first marriage was built on the sand.

The chances of a lasting marriage are greater if both spouses are focused on the Lord and they allow God to guide their lives on a daily basis. When the Lord is in our hearts and if we listen to our hearts, we will usually do what is right. The marriage license that is given to us, states that when you are married, you become one with God. This did not happen in my first marriage because we were not focused on God. I tried to share this with Pam, but she was not responsive, and ultimately the marriage did not last. Maybe now you can have a better understanding of why over 50% of marriages end in divorce.

It is so important to know your potential mate before you walk down the aisle or even before beginning a serious relationship, and particularly where the person stands with the Lord. Learn about his or her character and value system. Life brings us plenty of challenges, but an unhappy marriage is one we can avoid. I almost let my unhappy marriage destroy my life.

One must ask, "Do I want to live in confusion and pain, or do I want the joy the Lord can bring into my relationships?" I had one marriage without the Lord as the foundation, and I learned that didn't work. My second marriage has brought us challenges; nobody's life is perfect, but by focusing on the Lord, our lives together is much better. Kelly and I have worked very hard to maintain a life that doesn't include lies and deception. The Lord has truly blessed us.

I had to actually feel in my heart the pain that Jesus suffered on the cross to really understand about Jesus and God. Many times people who call themselves Christians realize it intellectually, but their hearts are not touched with His truth. Where do you stand? Is the Lord in your heart or only in your mind?

Thoughts for Reflection

- We need to learn to treat each other as Jesus would; our first thought should be how would He act or react in any given situation.

- Listen to your heart. God will speak to you. God will direct you.

- Lack of communication can cause an irreparable rift between two people. If you do not always know the right words to say, ask the Lord to help you with your words.

- We were all created by God. We all have a body, spirit and a mind. We have the choice to choose between living our lives in Darkness or in Lightness. Spiritual Lightness will make us a better person.

- Pray for your husband or wife and children. This will bring you closer to them.

Bible Verses for Study

Therefore everyone who hears these words of mine and puts them into practice is like a wise man who built his house on the rock. The rain came down, the streams rose and the winds blew and beat against that house; yet it did not fall because it had a foundation on the rock. But everyone who hears these words of mine and does not put them into practice is like a foolish man who built his house on sand. The rain came down, the streams rose, and the winds blew and beat against the house, and it fell with a great crash.

Matthew 7:24–27

"And when a great multitude were coming together, and those from the various cities were journeying to Him, He spoke by way of parable: The sower went out to sow his seed; and as he sowed, some fell beside the road; and it was trampled under foot, and the birds of the air ate it up. And other seed fell on rocky soil, and as soon as it grew up, it withered away, because it had no moisture. And the other seed fell among the thorns; and the thorns grew up with it, and choked it out. "And other seed fell into good soil, and grew up, and produced a crop a hundred times as great." As He said these things, He would call out, "He who has ears to hear, let him hear." And His disciples began questioning Him as to what this parable might be. And He said, "To you it has been granted to know the mysteries of the kingdom of God, but to the rest it is in parables, in order so that Seeing They May Not See, And Hearing They May Not Understand. "Now the parable is this: the seed is the word of God. "And those beside the road are those who have heard; then the devil comes and takes away the word from their heart, so that they may not believe and be saved. "And those on the rocky soil are those who, when they hear, receive the word with joy; and these have no firm root; they believe for a while, and in time of temptation fall away. "And the seed which fell among the thorns, these are the ones who have heard, and as they go on their way they are choked with worries and riches and pleasures of this life, and bring no fruit to maturity. "And the seed in good soil, these are the ones who have heard the word in an honest and good heart, and hold it fast and bear fruit with perseverance.

Luke 8:4–15

Unless the Lord builds the house, They labor in vain who build it; Unless the Lord guards the city, The watchman keeps awake in vain.

Psalm 127:1

Thy word is a lamp to my feet, And a light to my path.

Psalm 119:105

And so, as those who have been chosen of God, holy and beloved, put on a heart of compassion, kindness, humility, gentleness and patience; bearing with one another, and forgiving each other, whoever has a complaint against anyone; just as the Lord forgave you, so also should you. And beyond all these things put on love, which is the perfect bond of unity. And let the peace of Christ rule in your hearts, to which indeed you were called in one body; and be thankful.

Colossians 3:12–15

And knowing their thoughts He said to them, "Any kingdom divided against itself is laid waste; and any city or house divided against itself shall not stand.

Matthew 12:25

Questions

1. How can you standup for yourself when someone treats you in a poor manner?

2. How do you handle hurt, disappointment, and/or poor treatment from someone you know? Do you discuss the hurt or are you judgmental?

3. Why is it important for spouses to have a common spiritual relationship with the Lord in a marriage or even with friends?

4. Is the spirit of the Lord in your heart or only in your mind? Explain how you know He is truly in your heart.

5. What foundation would each of the following represent?

   A. Light + Light = Patience and Understanding in a Relationship

   B. Light + Dark = Confusion in a Relationship

   C. Dark + Dark = Possible Destruction in a Relationship

6. What foundation would you prefer to have in your family and in your life?

Sharing God's Love

When I found Jesus, my heart wanted to share this new experience with anyone who would listen, but I did not know how to be a disciple. The definition of disciple[2] is a pupil or follower who helps to spread his master's teachings or a member of the Disciples of Christ. After watching acquaintances and friends witnessing for the Lord, I realized witnessing would be difficult for me. I knew I had to find the right way for me to be a witness for the Lord. I knew that since God wanted me to share His love, He had already equipped me with the tools I would need. I just needed to be guided or shown my gift. I watched some friends set goals to witness to a particular number of people a day. They would talk to strangers and quote them Bible verses. At a point, they then would ask the person to pray with them, accepting Jesus Christ as their Savior. After seeing this type of witnessing I did not feel the Lord was directing me in this type of sharing. I prayed to the Lord to give me direction about the kind of witness He wanted me to be. His actions drew people to Him. People wanted to know more about Him. I wanted my actions and kindness to reflect my walk with the Lord and draw people to me. I was afraid if I witnessed like the friends I mentioned earlier, I would scare people away from the Lord. In my search for a way to witness, I watched Walt, who offered a helping hand. Walt was always kind and unassuming. His non-judgmental help had spoken to my heart. I observed some people in the church showed compassion simply by listening and talking with people. Each of us must depend on the Lord to direct us how to witness to someone. There is no wrong way if it is from the heart and is gracious. I will share with you a few of the ways I witness to people and ways others have witnessed to me over the years.

> *Let your speech always be with grace, seasoned, as it were, with salt, so that you may know how to respond to each person.*
>
> *Colossians 4:6*

During this time of searching for my personal way to witness, I was traveling on an interstate that was under construction. Because of the long delay on the road, I was forced to stop for gas. After pumping the gas, I went inside to pay the cashier. I noticed the young lady's name tag and called her by name. I went on to ask how her day was going. She seemed surprised by my question and asked me why I was being nice to her. I told her God wants us to say a kind word to a stranger. He wants us to be open and giving by showing His love through us. She said most of the people that came into the gas station were rude to her. I encouraged her to not let people's rudeness ruin her day.

Another time, I was taking a trip in my Corvette and had stopped to fill up with gas. An older gentleman stopped by my car to ask for a spare dollar or two. He commented on my nice car and how lucky I was to have such an expensive car. He had on his work clothes, so I asked him how his work was going. That opened the door for him to share with me. He said that he was not treated very well on his construction job and was struggling to keep it. I realized he was bitter, but had a feeling he was a hard worker. I told him that Jesus loves everyone and that no one should look down on him or treat him poorly. Usually when I mentioned the word of God or Jesus to someone that loves the Lord, they would speak up and give thanks. This man did not. I suggested he ask God to make changes in his life and at work in order for him to have peace. I suggested to him that if people kept treating him without respect, he could pray for them. Praying would soften his heart, and I already knew the miracles that can occur with an open heart. Before giving the man a couple of dollars, I shared with him that I, too, had been a construction worker. I also encouraged him to do his best in his job because his attitude could bring about changes in people that were giving him a hard time.

After I checked into a hotel during one of my business trips, I started to walk up the stairs to my room. I encountered a young woman sitting in the hotel stairwell. Just to be friendly, I asked her how she was doing. She said she was okay, but something in my heart told me she was not okay. I went on to my room with the intention of unpacking and settling in for the night. When I got there, I realized I had forgotten something in my truck and went back to get it. The woman was still sitting in the stairwell as I started down. Her demeanor made me feel a strong need to witness to her. I told her that something in my heart told me she was not doing well, and that she might want to talk to someone. She told me she was struggling with many things in her life. I mentioned I had written a spiritual story that I would like to share with her if she would read it. She said she would, and I asked her if God was in her life. Her answer was no but that an older, wiser friend had told her that she needed to depend on the Lord in order to straighten out her life. I looked straight into her eyes and said that I agreed with her friend and that she would soon be ready to depend on the Lord. Once I told her that, she began to tell me her troubles. She had married her high school sweetheart and had recently divorced. During their marriage they had three children together. Two of the children were living with her at the hotel. She was working two jobs trying to make ends meet. She had been evicted from her apartment because arguments with her ex-husband would escalate to violence and the police would be summoned to break up arguments. They divorced because her husband was having an affair and told her he did not love her anymore. In spite of the affair, she loved him and wanted him back. The tears came as she spoke; she was brokenhearted. I shared with her that I, too, had a very painful divorce and had a difficult time getting over my broken heart. I told her that once I found Jesus, He helped me get through that bad time. I told her He was still with me, helping me with difficult decisions in my life or when I stumble along life's path. I encouraged her to find Jesus so He could help her and change her spirit. If her spirit becomes kinder, more patient and more understanding, perhaps her ex-husband will see the change and want to know how it came about. If he is open to hearing what she has to say, they have a chance of working through their issues. I strongly believe the Lord can heal a broken marriage if both people make the decision to have Him heal the relationship. As I left to run my errand, I told her that I hoped she would let the Lord into her life while stressing to her that life would get better. During this time God placed the burning desire in my heart to share His story with this young lady.

> But if I say, "I will not remember Him Or speak anymore in His name," Then in my heart it becomes like a burning fire Shut up in my bones; And I am weary of holding it in, And I cannot endure it.
>
> Jeremiah 20:9

After fifteen years, the territory that I worked changed. The new area I covered was the hometown of Pam and her dad, Charlie. For four years I had no desire to contact Charlie, but recently I had felt like talking to him. Something in my heart had told me to write him. I wrote to Charlie, and I enclosed a sealed letter to Pam and asked him to give it to her. I told Charlie I needed to tell Pam how hurt I was from the divorce and what the Lord had meant to me in my life since the divorce. I also told Charlie that I had always looked up to him and loved him like a dad; I told him that I had lost more than Pam during the divorce. I missed being part of his family. I told him I was hesitant to call, so I decided to write first. He answered my letter, telling me that he loved me like a son still and that I was welcome to visit him any time. Lucy had, in fact, asked for a divorce and their marriage had ended. In my opinion, Lucy was the one that lost the most because she could not accept the Lord's truth and, therefore, lost her commitment to their marriage. In my heart I knew years ago that Lucy would not stay in the marriage unless she found the Lord.

I had hoped the letter to Pam would open the door for her to contact me. She told me once that life was too short, and one must get the most out of life. In the letter I tried to show her the way to get the most out of life was to live life God's way and to treat people the way she expected to be treated. I agreed that life is short, but we still have to deal with eternity. I have chosen to walk with Jesus Christ in my life. I said that I hoped the Lord had come into her life over the years and that she had His love. I hoped that she had found the peace and joy that she was searching for when we were married.

But to the rest I say, not the Lord, that if any brother has a wife who is an unbeliever, and she consents to live with him, let him not send her away.

I Corinthians 7:12

Yet if the unbelieving one leaves, let him leave; the brother or the sister is not under bondage in such cases, but God has called us to peace.

I Corinthians 7:15

I feel good about sharing this with Pam. I tried. It's been a struggle over the years because she did not allow me to meet with her. I wasn't able to ask her in person to forgive me for hurting her. I was hoping to hear she had grown with the Lord over the years, but I never heard from her. Pam probably just threw the letter I sent her into the trash. Jesus knows I did my best. I encourage all Christians to be a disciple for the Lord. Love the person, but hate the sin, not the person. She always said people couldn't change. I know people can change with Jesus in their hearts. When the Holy Spirit comes into our lives, hearts and souls, we become a better people. Since our divorce, Pam has been married twice and will probably marry again before her life is over if she does not find the Lord. She has not changed.

The Lord works in mysterious ways. The previous leader of the company I worked for almost destroyed the company by making bad decisions. The worst decision was trying to become the largest company in our industry while accumulating excessive debt during many ventures. He was asked to resign, and a new CEO took over. When the new CEO came on board, he was very concerned about the morale of his employees. He hired specially trained, independent consultants to discuss employee concerns with teams of employee representatives. This was to ensure that no one would feel intimidated to speak up. I was blessed to be part of one of the teams and had an opportunity to speak for our other employees.

I did not feel we were able to share factual information at the team meeting I attended. In preparation for the meeting, I prepared documentation with detailed information about our concerns. One of our concerns was that when our company was sold and merged with others over the years, most of our employees lost over 50% of the retirement benefits that were promised to us when we began work. Another concern was with the rising cost of our annual health insurance premiums. The company always told us they paid 70% of the cost of our benefits. I was able to compare another company's health care coverage with the same provider we used. Based on the cost comparison, our employees were paying much more for this benefit than the company claimed. At the end of the meeting, I requested the highest ranking company representative that attended to give our CEO the information I prepared. She stated she would gladly do so.

Once he reviewed the information, he responded positively by email. The main point he made was that reducing retirement benefits and passing on the high cost of insurance to the employees was a trend that started years back with many corporations. There was not much he could do about making changes at the time. He also mentioned

that this was "the realities of the world." In my response to
him, I conveyed that I had noticed during the first eight
months of his leadership of the company, he had tried
to make some good changes and that I felt he was asking God's advice for the decisions he had to make. In my
heart I knew by his actions he was a man of the Lord. I
thanked him for reading and reviewing the material. In
his next response by email, he confirmed that he did go to
church and that the Lord was a high priority in his life.
He shared a powerful lesson he heard at church Sunday,
which I will share with you:

> *The only thing we are charged with doing in this life
> is being disciples, and the way we measure success is to
> see how many disciples we create while we are trying
> to become one. The analogy used was as follows: As we
> plow, we need to look over our shoulder at what grows
> in the furrow we leave behind.*

Often when people cross our paths and we share the Lord
with them, we never see their growth with the Lord.
This message was very powerful to me because I feel the
plowed field is my marriage, and the seeds we plant are
our children. As I teach my son Matt about the Lord, I
can look back at his growth and be pleased in that I have
done my best. One must make the effort to be a teacher
to our children every day as well as others we need to
disciple. If I had not followed through on God's wish for
me to prepare the information for the CEO, I would have
missed a blessing and would have had regrets. The risk I

took was that I might have offended him. My faith in the Lord carried me down the path to speak.

Watching the news and driving on the interstate, I realized there were many people displaced from their homes because of the destruction left behind by hurricane Katrina. I could feel compassion for them because I once lived on the Mississippi Gulf Coast and had experienced several hurricanes. People's lives were in turmoil, and many had lost everything. The Lord placed it in my heart to share our basement apartment with a family. The least I could do was offer a little help. We found a family that needed help quickly. The basement apartment was designed so you could not access our upstairs living area. I felt comfortable with this, even though we did not really know very much about these people. After the family moved in, we realized they were not married. Later we found out they had their own separate apartments on the Gulf Coast. They had been married two previous times to each other and one time to someone else. They had two children together along with each of them having a child in their other marriages. The violence and destruction of the hurricane brought them together again. They were drawn to each other because of this dangerous time. They were never able to maintain a relationship with the Lord and, consequently, were never able to get their lives in order. I realized quickly that they had been living from paycheck-to-paycheck. They were really struggling to survive. A group of our friends from church came together to sponsor them with money, clothing, food, and moral support. Jobs were even offered. They had one son at home; the son was welcomed with open arms at our local school. He was well liked by everyone. They talked about rebuilding their lives together in our hometown since so many people were so gracious to them. As the weeks passed, when the opportunity presented itself, I asked them if they would like to read the story I was writing of my experiences. I encouraged them to depend on the Lord for their answers in these stressful times. Being away from other family members was overwhelming to them even though they said they would never go back to live on the Mississippi Gulf Coast because of the violent storm they had just experienced. Over the passing weeks, their relationship began to deteriorate. As each day passed, it seemed the stress became greater between them. After a little over two months, the tension became so great they departed separately. The mom and son came back a few weeks later to pick up their remaining belongings. The son thanked me for our help and made a comment about the story I had written. He said that he had read the whole story and it was great. He said it was sad that his mom and dad could not get their lives right together. I encouraged him that when he made a commitment to marriage be sure to have the Lord involved in their lives. It seemed the teenager had his life more together than his mom and dad.

College basketball playoffs usually occur during a month called March Madness. My son Matt loves to play basketball, football, and baseball. He is at the age of likening to watch sports on television. I suggested we see if a basketball game was on television. To my surprise, a channel was having a special about Pistol Pete Maravich, one of the greatest basketball players that ever played the game. He averaged 44.2 points a game during his college career and set many other records. He began practicing at a young age and practiced every day because he loved to play the game so much. Pistol Pete grew up with a basketball always in his hands. Since his dad was a college coach, he knew he wanted to play college ball.

He had a true gift and love for the sport and constantly worked hard to polish his skills. He was drafted to play professionally. Many say he was a solid professional ball player while others say he was one of the greatest to play professionally. The television special showed clips of him playing at different levels. I had flashbacks of seeing him play on television when he was in college and in the pros. I was still fascinated at how good he was. The Lord gave him the ability to play at the highest level, but Pistol Pete could not have accomplished this feat without hard work and practice. He had the heart and drive to become one of the best to play his sport. However, people that knew him throughout his life realized he was not a happy person. He was always searching for a different challenge to fill a void in his life. He retired from professional ball at the age of thirty-three, never playing on a winning national championship team in college or on a professional championship team. It's hard to believe with all he accomplished, Pistol Pete was not a happy person. He soon found out the void he was trying to fill was a spiritual one. After retiring from basketball, he accepted Jesus Christ as his Savior. He finally found the peace for which he was searching. Once this happened, he went around the country witnessing for the Lord by speaking at events. During basketball camps for children, he also talked about why everyone needs the Lord in his or her life. He witnessed to everyone that he could. He felt even though he accomplished so much playing basketball, the spiritual gift he found was greater. Sad to say, his life was cut short at the young age of forty while playing the game he loved. He was playing a pickup basketball game in a gym when he died of a massive heart attack. The autopsy indicated that only half of his heart worked from birth. Finding this out, everyone was amazed he had lived as long as he did with his heart condition. Life is short; we do not know when our time on earth will draw to an end. When we are younger, many times we act as though we will live forever and that we are invincible. At the end of Pistol Pete's life, he was truly a champion in God's eyes. During the special about Pistol Pete, Matt watched and listened intently. Afterward, I was able to talk with my son about the events in Pistol Pete's life while trying to teach Matt why the Lord is so important to depend on. It is better to have only one moment with the Lord than none! I have found that you can be a disciple to your child every day if you make the attempt.

> *All Scripture is inspired by God and profitable for teaching, for reproof, for correction, for training in righteousness; that the man of God may be adequate, equipped for every good work.*
>
> II Timothy 3:16–17

Others Witnessing

Over the years I have experienced friends and people having faith that the Lord can heal a disease or sickness. I have often doubted this could happen. Could I be a doubting Thomas? Doubting Thomas[3] is a term that is used to describe someone who refuses to believe something without direct, physical, personal evidence; a skeptic. The origin of the term is based on the Biblical account of Thomas the Apostle, who doubted the resurrection of Jesus and demanded to feel Jesus' wounds before being convinced (John 20:24–29); however, the Bible does not mention if actual physical contact took place between Jesus and Thomas. After seeing Jesus alive and being offered the opportunity to touch his wounds—according to the author of the Gospel of John— Thomas professed his faith in Jesus; on this account he is also called *Thomas the Believer*.

One day I was watching the Pat Robertson *700 Club*. He had a special guest, Daniel Thomas on his show. Daniel talked about being diagnosed with cerebral palsy as a child. Growing up Daniel experienced muscle spasms, his speech was not clear, and even when taking medication he would have eight seizures a day; plus in addition he suffered with epilepsy. This was not easy for him to face as a child or as an adult. He could not function normally. Cerebral palsy is caused by brain damage; there is no known cure. Through all of this he had the spirit and the drive to finish high school. As an adult, Daniel accepted the Lord as his Savior; he studied the Bible and began to realize the Lord could heal his broken body. He was in constant prayer for a miracle for the Lord to heal him; he had faith the Lord could do this for him. One night at church, a church member prayed for him to be healed; Daniel felt electricity go through his body. People around him immediately noticed his facial features were not as constricted. Something was happening, he was changing. From that moment, his physical abilities began to improve; with time and through prayer, the seizures disappeared. Believe it: Daniel is driving and playing the guitar. He is enjoying life as he dreamed for many years. The story line for the segment was *If You Just Believe*. This was a miracle and a blessing from God. Through Daniel's faith, being a disciple for the Lord, and sharing his story has given me more faith. The Lord can heal us in today's time. Our God is powerful. As we grow in the knowledge of the Lord, we get a better understanding and a stronger faith in what the Lord can really do for us. We need to open our hearts, to listen and to *Believe*!

Many times we are unaware of the effect we have when witnessing for the Lord. So, it is rewarding to know when it has had a positive effect. A close friend of mine called one day and excitedly told me that he had shared two copies of my story with two of his friends that did not have a relationship with the Lord. Neither of them had ever been involved in a church. My friend Karl said he received a phone call from one of his friends who had read my story. His friend had opened his heart to the words of the story and told Karl that he had accepted Jesus Christ as his Savior! Since opening his heart to the Lords words and spirit, his life has changed. At the age of fifty-five, he has become involved in church for the first time. This shows us it is never too late. What a blessing I felt to know that someone opened his heart to the Lord's words!

It is hard for many people to witness for the Lord. More

of the family of Christ should respond to His commandment to go and make disciples of all nations and share their
story with others. Tommy, an acquaintance and a state
trooper, and I were talking one day when I mentioned the
Lord. I knew he was dedicated to his job and was a caring
person towards all people. Often when dealing with people
on his job, he has seen a tremendous amount of violence
and the dark side of people's lives. When I mentioned the
Lord, he boldly spoke up and told me he wanted to share a
special story with me.

One night Tommy was driving in a mountainous rural
area when he came upon a vehicle with five men in the
car. They slowed the car down to five miles per hour when
they saw him behind them. Normally that late at night a
car full of guys would indicate trouble could come quickly
to Tommy if he stopped them. Tommy was curious. While
reaching to turn the siren and blue lights on, he heard a
voice in the back seat saying, "Tommy do not stop the
car." He looked in the back seat, and no one was there.
He reached down again to turn on the lights and siren,
and the voice came from the front seat, this time in a
deeper tone, "Tommy do not stop the car." In spite of this,
he was still going to do his job. The third time he heard
the voice it spoke so loudly that the windows in his car
shook. At that point Tommy pulled his car off the road.
His legs were shaking so badly he couldn't drive. While he
sat on the side of the road trying to calm down, he began
to reflect on an incident that had happened a few weeks
prior to this dark night. He had stopped a motorist that
was speeding who happened to be a minister. The minis-

ter admitted he had been speeding, he knew it was wrong and graciously took the ticket. Before taking off again, he asked Tommy if he would pray with him. Tommy agreed, and during the prayer, the minister asked the Lord to provide an angel to watch over him. Now Tommy realized that the voice was God's angel watching over him. His life had probably just been saved by the voice he heard. It made sense to him that those men would have proved very dangerous to approach, and he might have been killed. He was in an isolated rural area at night and would not have been able to get any help. It took Tommy only a minute to accept that prayer is powerful and that God does exist. Wow! What a powerful witness for the Lord! Your experience does not have to be so "wow," but the key is to share your life's experiences and show people you do care about them.

After these encounters, I thanked God that He allowed people like this to cross my path and others to witness to me. I prayed they would see Jesus in me. I could see Jesus in others' lives. I prayed for God's wisdom and guidance concerning my witnessing. By God allowing me to witness to these people I can see God was showing me the gift He had given me. I do not know if these people came to accept the Lord, but perhaps my actions planted the seed of God in their hearts. God's promise is that the seeds will grow to fruition and the lives of these people will be changed; thus, in turn, they will be able to share God's love, thus, increasing the Lord's disciples. Would Jesus not witness and care for all people?

Thoughts for Reflection

- Be a disciple for the Lord. Share your love and story with all people when the opportunity arises. Your story may be just a kind word spoken to a stranger.

- Share your love of the Lord; we must be bold for Christ in a kind way. Do not be overbearing.

- The way you treat someone can have a negative lasting impact on his or her life. Be kind to all people because God loves everyone. You can make a difference in someone's life even if it is just for a moment.

- Walking with the Lord will allow you to live a better, more disciplined life with value and sharing.

- God wants us to be content in life instead of searching in many directions for happiness. I have found contentment in knowing Jesus Christ.

- I have come to realize that things happen in my life in His timing, not my timing. Could it be that He wants me to be happy with my life each day while not searching for happiness tomorrow?

- I feel that Jesus walked on earth to show us that there is a heavenly Father. We must realize and accept this before we become a child of God.

Bible Verses for Study

And walking by the Sea of Galilee, He saw two brothers, Simon who was called Peter, and Andrew his brother, casting a net into the sea; for they were fishermen. And He said to them, "Follow Me, and I will make you fishers of men."

Matthew 4:18–19

And I say to you, everyone who confesses Me before man, the Son of Man shall confess him also before the angels of God; but he who denies Me before men shall be denied before the angels of God.

Luke 12:8–9

And when the scribes of the Pharisees saw that He was eating with the sinners and tax-gatherers, they began saying to His disciples, "Why is He eating and drinking with tax-gatherers and sinners?" And hearing this, Jesus said to them, "It is not those who are healthy who need a physician, but those who are sick; I did not come to call the righteous, but sinners."

Mark 2:16–17

I SOLEMNLY charge you in the presence of God and of Christ Jesus, who is to judge the living and the dead, and by appearing and His kingdom: preach the word; be ready in season and out of season; reprove, rebuke, exhort, with great patience and instruction.

II Timothy 4:1–2

Finally brethren, pray for us that the word of the Lord may spread rapidly and be glorified, just as it did also with you; and that we may be delivered from perverse and evil men; for not all have faith.

But the Lord is faithful, and He will strengthen and protect you from the evil one.

II Thessalonians 2:1–3

Questions

1. Can you think of ways that you can share or show God's love?

2. Is it better to be humble or overbearing when trying to lead someone to Christ?

3. What gifts/talents has God given you, and have you been using them to the fullest?

4. Unfortunately statistics show over 50% of marriages end in divorce. I can bet many times one person comes to the conclusion in their marriage that they do not love their life partner anymore. Has this happened to you in a marriage or a relationship, and if so, why?

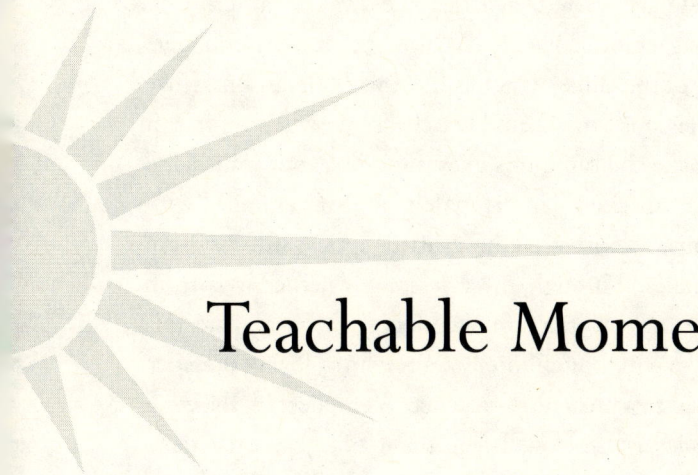

Teachable Moments

We have opportunities everyday to teach and share our knowledge with our children. We must take advantage of every opportunity today because we do not know what tomorrow will bring. Often, we get too busy; we are preoccupied with our work, home projects, television, computer stuff, and life's worries. As a result, we do not appropriate quality time our children deserve and need. With everything going on in our lives, we are often too tired to make the effort. It is hard to find balance in our lives for everything we need to accomplish in a day's time. Being blessed with a child later in life has made me even more aware of what the Lord wants in my life for my son. It is my duty as a parent to be a disciple to him. I need to spend quality time as well as a quantity of my time with him having fun. If I do not take the time to do so, in the end I will have wasted my time on earth as a father.

Through God's love He has brought me a better understanding of the Bible, which is filled with life lessons. If we take the lessons from the Bible to heart, we will be more apt not to make the same mistakes. God does not want us to repeat our mistakes. Unfortunately our lives are filled with life lessons; too often we have learned the hard way from our mistakes. Through these lessons, whether it is from the Bible or from our life experiences, we can share this knowledge with our children in a teaching, loving presence as opposed to a preaching presence. As I reflect on the verse from Ecclesiastes below, I feel it is my duty as a parent to share my knowledge about God, to teach His foundation for life to my son. If I do not, I will have wasted the opportunity. I would like to share with you ways that I have tried to teach and share wisdom with my son.

> *If a man fathers a hundred children and lives many years, however many they be, but the soul is not satisfied with good things, and he does not even have a proper burial, then I say, "Better the miscarriage than he."*
> Ecclesiastes 6:3

I experienced a tremendous blessing while trying to introduce my son to Sunday school. Since we wanted our beautiful son to be involved in Sunday school, we began taking him to our new church after we moved. Matt did not want me to leave him in Sunday school, maybe because I had to travel for my job during the week. So I stayed and got involved in his class. The same teacher taught every Sunday, and when she saw how interested I was in helping the children, she asked me if I would alternate teaching every other Sunday with her so she could have some time off. Matt was four years old at the time, and I gladly accepted the offer. Before I realized it, I was teaching every Sunday. One Sunday our minister stopped by class and expressed how surprised and pleased he was that there was a male role model for the children in Sunday school. My efforts were returned many times over by the excitement and love of the children. Often I see husbands and wives teaming up to teach Sunday school lessons which show our youth the importance of God being present in the family.

God has commissioned men to be the spiritual leaders in our churches and our homes. Fulfilling this commission has always been hard for me. I often struggle with going to church, but I know I need the support of other Christians during worship times as well as outside church. This helps me stay focused on the Lord.

As a parent, I feel the need to teach my child about the Bible and the love of the Lord. I believe children need a strong religious foundation when they are young to help them deal with the many negative temptations and negative people they will encounter growing up and to help them with decision-making later on in life as well. It is important to introduce them at an early age to the Ten Commandments, especially God's greatest two commandments and the stories in the children's Bible. In particular, I have shared with my son Matt the ones dealing with respecting our parents and not lying. I have also told him that he needs to treat people the way he would want to be treated. To make the commandments more personal I asked Matt if he would like to be lied to or disrespected. As our children get older, parents can go into more depth about other commandments. We need to teach our children that when we do not live by God's laws, we will face negative consequences. We should take every opportunity to praise children for doing something right or to explain why something they did was wrong.

Children need loving discipline and guidance. I believe that Jesus calls parents to train by example with extreme patience. Children depend on us to do so. They should not be screamed at, belittled, or beaten down when they make mistakes. Discipline is a part of love we have for our children, and if handled correctly, can build a child's self-esteem and character. God wants us to take the time when disciplining our children to share His commandments and His wisdom with them.

> *And you shall love the Lord your God with all your heart and with all your soul and with all your might. "And these words, which I am commanding you today, shall be on your heart; and you shall teach them diligently to your sons and shall talk of them when you sit in your house and when you walk by the way and when you lie down and when you rise up. "And you shall bind them as a sign on your hand and they shall be as frontals on your forehead. And you shall write them on the doorposts of your house and on your gates.*
>
> Deuteronomy 6:5–9

I have tried to show Matt the consequences that people face

when they make fun of or emotionally abuse others. Abusers push people away. They will find themselves alone, without friends or respect. In the end, by treating others in ungodly ways, we hurt ourselves. When my son and I encounter someone being cruel or mean, I ask Matt, "Would you want to be treated like that?" The different perspective allows him to understand this commandment better.

A friend at school the other day was talking with Matt and called him fat. This hurt his feelings. He is a big kid, but not fat. His arms and legs are very big and strong for his age. During this time he was in the fourth grade; his legs are the same diameter as mine; they are nothing but muscle. Pound for pound, he is stronger than I. I can tell this by wrestling with him; I would be in big trouble if he were my size; I would never win. I told him that I did not consider him fat, and that when he has a growth spurt, his weight will be just right. It is amazing to see a child's growth each year from the physical and intelligential phases of his or her life. It is a blessing to share my love, give him the support he needs, and see him grow every day. Since that incident, I have tried to show him why it is so important to think how another person feels when a personal comment is directed at them. I have encouraged Matt to stand up for anyone being treated in a cruel manner. I promised to support him every time he does so. I made time to reaffirm the consequences if I ever heard him being cruel to someone else. This kind of behavior is not acceptable nor will it be tolerated in our family. Every person is special in God's eyes, regardless of their physical appearance.

When disciplining a child, our rules must be clear and

consistent. Changing the rules and consequences only confuse the child.

> *Therefore, however you want people to treat you, so treat them, for this is the Law and the Prophets.*
>   Matthew 7:12

The other day I picked Matt up from a friend's house where he had been playing for a few hours after school. His friend's mother, Belinda, told me that before getting home, they stopped by another friend's house. Her daughter, Maggie; her son, Harrison; and Matt went to the back yard to play for a few minutes. While Belinda was talking to her friend, she thought she heard rocks splashing in the water of the goldfish pond. Afraid that the fish would be hurt, she went around back to see what was going on. She asked Harrison and Matt if they had been throwing rocks in the pond. They denied that they had. She then asked Maggie, who said that they had all been throwing rocks. Harrison quickly admitted the truth, but Matt continued to deny it. On the way home, I asked Matt again if he were throwing rocks into the goldfish pond. I was pleased this time he immediately admitted to participating in the rock throwing. Why, I asked him, did he lie to Mrs. Belinda. He said he was scared about the punishment Mrs. Belinda would have given him. I told Matt that he had been wrong to lie, and he would now have to face the consequences which would be worse than telling the truth from the beginning. Tomorrow night, I said, we would go to Mrs. Belinda's house and he would have to apologize for lying to

her. Then he would have to apologize to Harrison. I'm sure
he would rather have had a whipping than the embarrass-
ment of facing up to his lying. I went into detail about why
God does not want us to lie and that we should act with
honor and integrity. I told him if he could not get the words
out with an apology to both of them, he would not be able
to play in his basketball game this coming weekend. He
would have to go to the game and sit on the bench while I
helped coach his team. This would be his punishment. This
really bothered him since he is the team leader and one of
the best players on his church league team. It was difficult
for him to apologize, but he did do it. This was an example
of taking advantage of an opportunity to teach an important lesson. If I had not shown Matt the consequences of
his actions, he would think that lying is okay and it might
become a regular habit.

The definition of *discipline*[4] is "training that develops
self-control and character." As Christian parents, we must
train our children in the ways of the Lord. Godly discipline
results in building a child's spirit with honesty and integrity.
I have noticed that when I teach Matt about God, his spirit
is more loving and caring. During the training of my son I
try to help him understand that God will speak to him, and
that he should listen to his heart because God often directs
us through our conscience, which tells us right from wrong.
I believe that many of us do not take time to listen to God.
We will never find God's will unless we pay attention to the
many ways He may direct us.

When my son has done something wrong, my wife
and I ask him what his heart said before he followed

through with his actions. He has answered that he knew it was wrong. We explain the importance of listening to that inner voice, and we praise him for being honest with us. We also continue to allow him to feel the consequences of his actions. As a parent, I know that we should be calm when disciplining our children. However, sometimes it is very hard to maintain calm. I strive to be a parent that disciplines with love and compassion, yet I make mistakes. The other day Matt was asking the same question over and over again, and I had already told him why he could not have company over to the house. After the third time he asked to have company, I raised my voice and slammed my hand on the kitchen table. I quickly realized I had hurt his feelings. I went to him and apologized for raising my voice in anger. I told him it was wrong for me to hurt his feelings like that. I knew I should have sat down with him and taken more time with him to explain why he could not have a friend over. My simple apology proved to be a tremendous example to him. Children learn from our words and our actions. Each child is different and what works with one may not necessarily work with another. It is important to find the right way to reach your child even if you must ask the advice of an expert.

Everyone wants his or her children to thrive in life. We especially do not want them to hurt others or to be hurt. The best way to protect children is by teaching them about God. It is our duty and privilege to be able to share our knowledge and wisdom with our sons and daughters. Telling them about a few of our own mistakes in life shows them that we speak from experience and not just from a book. If we can give our children examples of faith in God's love and wisdom, then we have done a good job. Faith will be an important tool in dealing with adult issues when they are living on their own. Life brings many challenges to overcome, and every one that we conquer makes us stronger.

Some children seem to have a clear sense of right and wrong. I've noticed that Matt will let me know when I've made a mistake. God states in the Bible that parents need to train their children in His word. As a parent, I try to love and cherish Matt everyday. Ideally, both parents should work together to teach children about God. Through this teaching we are showing them how to communicate and share not only with God, but with other people as well. A family is one of God's greatest blessings to me, and I want my son to know that I consider him a blessing. Through my faith in God, I have a deeper understanding of life.

> *Train up a child in the way he should go, Even when he is old he will not depart from it.*
> Proverbs 22:6

Opportunities to teach our children occur at the most unexpected times. The other night Matt and I were wrestling and watching television. I was flipping through the channels when I came across a Christian show. Matt had never wanted to watch this show, so I suggested we watch it for a minute. Once he got interested in the story, he couldn't leave until it was over. He wanted to wrestle only during commercials. The story was about a middle-aged man in jail facing death. He was scheduled to die in three days. In the adjoining jail cell was a teenager that had just committed a gang-related murder and was very bitter about life. The older man had also been a gang member once. He had a wife and two sons that he had left many years ago and hadn't seen since. After a time of listening to the young man in the next cell, he realized that the teenager was his eldest son. He told him who he was and apologized to him for not being around to be a father to him while sharing that he had accepted Jesus Christ during his time on death row. Jesus Christ had replaced the rage within this man with peace. Part of the message in this show was that it is never too late to accept the Lord. The man scheduled to die asked his son to urge his younger brother not to follow in their footsteps. The father wanted to end the cycle of gang violence in their family. Matt asked me why they got involved in gangs and why they were both so angry. I told Matt that the old man's father probably left him at a young age, so he had turned to gangs for male support. I speculated that they were angry because that is what was shown to them growing up in their family and in gang life. Their anger, their violence, and their tempers caused them to commit crimes that brought them to jail. Both the dad and son knew in their hearts before committing their crimes that what they were about to do was wrong. Instead of listening to their conscience, they went ahead with their plan.

This was one of those teachable moments, so I took a moment to reflect on Matt's temper. I told Matt that his mother and I were concerned about the way he expressed his anger. I explained that when he lost his temper, he could seriously hurt someone. Then I asked him how he would like to spend his life in a jail cell and lose his freedom. Obviously, he did not want to end up there. He loves his freedom and big bed. God gave me that opportunity to teach my son this lesson. I also used this moment to talk about how Jesus wants us to treat other people. Matt was touched by the show and seemed to understand the importance of following God's instructions for our lives. It is often hard for children to grasp the understanding of God and His Son, so witnessing to our children is a special privilege that God has given parents. God expects us to teach our children His ways.

The other night after supper I was working on this story; Matt came over and sat in my lap. He asked if he was in the story. When I told him he was, he wanted to know why. I told him that I prayed daily for the Lord to show me what to write about and He had made it clear that I should include Matt in the story. Matt wanted to know why God wanted me to talk about him in the story. I told Matt that I believed God was directing me to share how we live in our family with others who may need encouragement or direction. Since this story is about my journey with God and my son is part of my life, he has a definite place in the story. Matt immediately wanted to know when he could read the story. I told him since there are a lot of grown-up struggles in my story; he should wait until he is older. Later that evening he reached over and gave me a hug. Sharing God's love and instructions with Matt seems to make him more open and loving. That night after Matt had been sleeping for an hour or so, he woke up in a panic calling me. I ran upstairs and asked him what was wrong. He said that he had a nightmare about a werewolf. I told him to pray for God to be there and tell the wolf to go away. Matt wanted to shoot the werewolf, but I told him God could do a better job. Sometimes parents are not sure their words get through to their children. This was one of those times! I wanted desperately to show Matt how to depend on the Lord in his life.

Just when I doubt Matt is getting the message, he surprises me by showing me that he does understand what I mean. This happened while we were building our home. When we decided to move, we thought it would be a good idea to build our home ourselves, and we made a special point of including Matt in many aspects of the project. He rode on the tractors with me, hammered nails, and played in the sand and gravel piles. He thought it was neat to live in the basement while we were finishing the upstairs. He even thought it was an adventure to sleep on a mattress on the floor. When it was time to finish his bathroom, we encouraged him to pick his own fixtures and shower inserts. Part of this project was to show Matt that God gives us blessings in life. One of my blessings is the ability to build houses. My wife and I wanted Matt to know that with God's help everything is possible. About a year after we finished our home, Matt and I were walking down the driveway when he stopped to ask me a question. He wanted to borrow my tools to build a home for his family when he gets older. I was delighted that he wanted to do that, and I told him that I hoped I could help him build his first home. Feeling that he had been an integral part of the building of his home gave him a sense of accomplishment and confidence in himself.

Matt has often asked me what I thought about him becoming a doctor, fireman, policeman, or even a professional athlete. I tell him that with God as the center of his life, he can do anything. He could even be President of the United States if that's the direction he feels God is leading him. The most important thing when it comes to making a life-changing decision is to listen to his heart and pray for God's guidance. He has God-given talents, which he should show appreciation for by working hard in school and applying himself in anything he attempts. I've stressed that God wants us to have a balanced life. Do you struggle with all work and no play? I do. I hope that Matt remembers to enjoy the life that God has given him. It was important for me to make Matt aware that as a young person I did not always follow God's lead. As a result, I faced many hard times.

My son made the all-star baseball team at the age of nine. He plays third base, short stop and pitcher. This was a great accomplishment since he broke his arm at the start of last season playing football against a fourteen year-old neighbor. It is common for him to ask me to practice with him by throwing and hitting the ball. I feel it is very important to make the time to practice with him. I want him to use his abilities to the best of his capabilities when he decides to play a sport. When he does his best, it helps his confidence and self-esteem. It is easy to discern the kids that do not practice. Sports can teach a child about team work, perseverance, sportsmanship, the value of hard work and dealing with adversity.

Another teachable moment came during the all-star series. In one game my son made three defensive plays that I did not think he would make. For a nine year-old he looked like a professional making the difficult plays. The third base coach for the other team walked out on the field to congratulate him on his successful play. I thanked the coach for doing this; his reply was that any kid that could make those plays deserves a high five even if he plays for the other team. Coaches and parents need to realize that young ball players can look like a professional at times and look like their age while making other plays. When they make a bad play, we need to show them what they did wrong in a positive manner and then encourage them to make the play the next time they have the opportunity. In our next game we needed to win the game to keep playing in the tournament. Both teams were playing well. During the game the umpires did make four bad calls against our team. It was frustrating for our players, the coaches, and the parents. You hope in a case like this the bad calls balance out for both teams, but in this game it did not. The game went into extra innings and the game ended with a close play. The play was a questionable call by the umpire. It ended with the other team winning. A few of coaches and a few of the dads showed their frustrations in front of the players by downing the umpires' bad calls. On the way home, Matt showed his frustrations toward the umpires, which gave me the opportunity to talk about life. I tried to show him that life is not always fair and things do not always turn out as we would like. I tried to show him that being a referee or umpire is very difficult; they do make mistakes in making calls. This is part of the game. You hope the calls balance out. I showed him that the best thing you can do is work harder to make the catch quicker by charging the ball and throwing it a little bit quicker so there will not be a close play. Maybe next year when he plays baseball again, he can encourage his team mates to make the plays quicker so they will not be in a situation to have close plays. During this simple lesson, I was trying to teach my son about how to face adversity, along with guiding him to become a better ball player.

> *I can do all things through Christ who strengthens me.*
>
> Philippians 4:13

> *Listen, O my people, to my instructions; Incline your ears to the words of my mouth. I will open my mouth in a parable; I will utter dark sayings of old. Which we have heard and known. And our fathers have told us. We will not conceal them from their children, But tell to the generation to come the praises of the Lord, And His strength and His wondrous works that He has done. For He established a testimony in Jacob, them to their children, That the generation to come might know, even the children yet to be born, That they may arise and tell them to their children, That they should put their confidence in God, And not forget the works of God, But keep His commandments.*
>
> Psalm 78:1–7

Baseball - The Greatest American Pastime Sport

Another opportunity came up to witness to my son the other day. During football season we are bad about flipping channels to see what other games are televised. We came across a special story about an all-pro football player, Corey Dillon. We stopped flipping the channels to watch. Corey was rated as one of the top three running backs in the country his junior year. He decided since he was rated so high, he would declare himself eligible for the upcoming draft. He thought he would be a sure high number one draft pick. During the draft, he was not chosen in the first round; he was drafted in the second round. He could not understand why; he was hurt after being told by many he would be a sure number one pick. It sounded as though the teams were told he did not deserve to be selected in the first round because of his attitude and would not be worth a gamble to be taken as a first rounder. It is important to make good grades, play/work hard while having a good attitude, along with staying out of trouble. Your reputation can hurt you if you do not conduct yourself in a positive way off the field.

While it was disappointing being taken in the second round, Corey used the hurt in a positive way to drive himself harder to perform and excel. He had the desire to overcome. Corey told many of his friends and family that his goal was to become rookie of the year and to show teams that bypassed him that they were wrong for not drafting him. This drive made him work harder, and he was selected rookie of the year. Even with this accomplishment, along with making more money than he ever dreamed he would, he was still missing something in his life. Many times people try to fill their spiritual emptiness with things such as spending many hours in bars drinking with friends, which Corey did. The drinking can lead us down the wrong path while pushing us toward wrong decisions. Even though Corey met a beautiful lady and started a family with her, he was not happy. During this time he attended church with his girlfriend and child. One Sunday Corey was sitting in the back of the church; the minister made a call for anyone that would like to accept the Lord to come to the front of the church. At that time he felt his chest tighten while the Lord was telling him that it was his time to accept Jesus Christ. It took a few moments to begin the walk up front, but he did accept Christ that day. It changed his life forever. He lost the passion to go to bars. Corey married his beautiful girl-friend and began truly living for the Lord. After the show I placed my hand on my son's chest as I stated one day the Lord may place that desire in your heart. You never know when He will knock on your soul!

> *And the world is passing away, and also its lust; but*
> *the one who does the will of God abides forever.*
>
> I John 2:17

I often use my mistakes or others' mistakes in the hope of teaching Matt to avoid those same errors. Over the holidays, two teenagers that live in our area decided to have a few drinks while they were driving around town one night. There was a terrible accident. The passenger of the car died in the accident. Both of the teenagers were intoxicated. The driver of the car is now facing manslaughter charges. What happened to these boys was horrifying to me as a parent since I couldn't help but imagine how I would feel if one of them had been Matt. I pray that Matt will turn to God when he is faced with this type of situation. I know that parents cannot watch over or be with their children twenty-four hours a day. My prayer is that my teaching over the years will open Matt's heart to God so that he may use His guidance when making decisions. I want my son to be strong enough to be a leader and make the right decisions. I wanted Matt to understand that the decision these two boys made didn't ruin only their lives,

but also their actions devastated two families. I stressed to
him that every choice we make has consequences. I told
Matt if he is not sure whether what he is about to do is not
right, he should ask God. He will always direct your heart,
if you ask. I cannot stress enough to Matt the importance
of standing and making the right choice, even if it means
going against his friends. We must teach our children that
they are to take responsibility for their actions and not to
blame someone else.

> *'For I know the plans that I have for you,' declares the
> Lord, 'plans for welfare and not for calamity to give
> you a future and a hope. 'Then you will call upon Me
> and come and pray to Me, and I will listen to you.
> 'And you will seek Me and find Me, when you search
> for Me with all your heart. 'And I will be found by
> you,' declares the Lord, 'and I will restore your fortunes
> and will gather you from all the nations and from all
> the places where I have driven you,' declares the Lord,
> 'and I will bring you back to the place from where I
> sent you into exile.'*
>
> Jeremiah 29:11–14

Life is Over in an Instant if You Make a Critical
Mistake—Have You Lost a Friend

As Matt gets older, he is learning about life through the way children interact with each other. At school Matt and a buddy were talking about the sports magazine they like to read. A third boy spoke up saying that he did not think it was fun to read about sports. This child continued to annoy Matt and the other boy by making fun of them. Guess what happen then? My son told the boy to shut up. Matt's teacher heard the word shut up and asked who said it. The third boy spoke up quickly and said it was Matt. After Matt got into trouble, one of the boys told Matt to shut up, aggravating him more. He could not understand why the other boy did not get into trouble. Kelly found out what happened and shared this with me. Since

Matt felt bad enough about the incident, I decided to wait another day to talk about the wording he used. The following day while driving to baseball practice, I told him his mom informed me he had a tough day at school. He told me why he used the word *shut up*. Many times the kids make fun of him when he is polite and uses the words *be quiet;* because it was not cool. I told him in many cases when kids or adults are cruel, he needs to ignore them, realizing that they do not have his best interest at heart. I suggested he walk away from a situation like this and say nothing. I asked him did he feel better after telling the boy to shut up or did he feel bad. He stated he felt bad about it, but he added that I did not understand what he was going through at his age. I told him that I was once his age and I do understand. I asked Matt, "Would Jesus tell someone to shut up?" Matt stated Jesus would not tell someone to shut up. Matt is beginning to understand how tough it is to do the right thing. What Jesus would have us do is not what society considers the coolest behavior.

Most children that play sports have dreams of playing at higher levels. When I played ball, I dreamed of playing football for the Green Bay Packers. My son is no different than I and others. Knowing that he wants to play at a higher level, I told him he needs to practice and play as much as he can to develop his skills to become a better ball player. An individual must have the drive to develop skills on his or her own. You must have the desire to play; you must have passion and love for the game to be successful. Parents cannot make their children go and run to increase their speed and agility. We cannot make them shoot basketball to increase their accuracy. We cannot make them work out with weights to gain more strength, etc. An athlete has to make a choice to do extra conditioning and practice on his or her own to be able to achieve more. I was an athlete who started to prepare for a season right before it started. Other priorities in life did not allow me to become a better athlete in the game I loved; so the result was I did not play at higher levels. As parents, we must help our children find a balance in training and playing sports along with having fun doing other things. I have shared with Matt that I feel God has given him the ability to play at higher levels, but he must use and train those gifts. Since he has dreams of playing ball professionally, I asked him how many of his friends did he think would make it to the majors. His answer was ten. I had to break the bad news to him that only one may make it. He could now relate to how competitive sports are at the highest level. We know only one professional baseball player from our area; with this he can relate to the number only being one. I told him that no matter what direction God leads him, we will support him.

As a parent I feel, we need to teach our children to have a spiritual foundation, expect them to do their best in school, and support them in all activities to help them become successful. As parents we can help our children find their God-given *gifts, talents, and abilities.* Parents need to savor and enjoy the time they have with their children. We have opportunities everyday to teach and share our lives with our children. We need to keep them as a top priority on our "to-do list"! Kelly and I do savor the moments with our son.

Thoughts for Reflection

- As parents, it is our responsibility to help our children find the gifts, talents, and abilities God has given them. Through this we are able to teach them His ways. In the end, it will be their choice which path they take.

- When you see someone doing something wrong, encourage him or her to do what is right in a godly way.

- Children need discipline in their lives. Be direct and do not give in. Discipline children in a godly way.

- If you find yourself screaming at any of your family members, consider how you would feel being screamed at in that manner. Control your actions or your reactions. You are hurting the feelings of someone that loves you, and in the end, you are only hurting yourself.

- Love and cherish each moment and day your child is in your life. Spend quality and quantity of time with them. Before you realize they will be grown and on their own.

Bible Verses for Study

Behold, children are a gift of the Lord; The fruit of the womb is a reward.

Psalm 127:3

I thank my God always concerning you, for the grace of God which was given you in Christ Jesus, that in everything you were enriched in Him, in all speech and all knowledge, even as the testimony concerning Christ was confirmed in you, so that you are not lacking in any gift, awaiting eagerly the revelation of our Lord Jesus Christ.

I Corinthians 1:4–7

As each one has received a special gift, employ it serving one another, as good stewards of the manifold grace of God.

I Peter 4:10

And because you are sons, God has sent forth the Spirit of His Son into our hearts, crying "Abba! Father!" Therefore you are no longer a slave, but a son; if a son, then an heir through God.

Galatians 4:6–7

Questions

1. How can discipline and having a spiritual foundation lead to self control?

2. What are your thought/reactions to a person that has a negative or demeaning attitude?

3. Are you a teacher and a disciple in your children's lives?

4. As parents how can we encourage our children's talents?

5. Are you using your gifts and talents the way God wants?

6. As a child or teenager, were you taught about the way you should live your life spiritually? If so, list the people that impacted and shaped your life.

7. What are we teaching our children when we belittle and scream at our spouse and/or children? Does this show self-control or weakness?

8. What happens in most cases when our youth are not taught or shown how to live their lives based on a spiritual foundation?

Expectations

When families raise their children in their church and a child is baptized, we are asked as a congregation to support each child in the way Jesus would want us to. The support we pledge to the children involves showing respect for one another, courtesy to all, positive discipline when needed, guidance through the rough spots, but most of all, we pledge our love, just as God pledges His love for us. Even if you do not believe in the spiritual foundation of God, I bet you want the same for your child. Since we cannot be with our children all of the time, we depend on other people to guide them in their walk. We depend on others while our children are at day care, at school, sporting events, dance classes, Boy Scouts, Girl Scouts and many other places. We depend on many individuals to use appropriate guidance with our children. If we see other adults not doing as they should, we can voice our concerns to the person responsible. If they continue to display behavior in opposition to our beliefs, we, as parents, have the responsibility to remove our child from their supervision. We should not allow negative behaviors to influence our children because they will learn that such behavior is acceptable.

I would like to share my family's experiences with several youth baseball teams, and see which team you would rather be involved with. I was excited when my son was asked to play on a team that had some of the best ball players from our area. This team played two or three weekends a month in tournament events. The team would play four or five games during the weekend. My son played on this coach's team previously, and we were apprehensive about the leadership of the team, but we wanted our son to have the experience of a competitive team. The coach was proud to say he would not curse or physically touch a player. He also boasted that he was an excellent coach and told us all about his winning record.

At the beginning of the season, the coach and I had a disagreement. I stood my ground. I told him that his attitude toward the parents and boys was terrible. It was not worth playing on his team under these conditions. He apologized and stated he still wanted my son to play. With the apology, I stated that I would give his team another chance. However, I felt his apology had no depth. I truly thought I could be a positive influence on the head coach by staying with the team and encouraging him to treat the boys better. In telephone conversions with him, I tried to encourage him to be more positive with the players. In one phone conversation, he stated that if he makes a player cry over a mental mistake or an error, that player would probably not make that same mistake again. I stressed to him on several occasions the players are only children, not professionals. In one of our conversations he pointed out something he felt I was doing wrong. I thought about it with an open mind and agreed with his direction. I thanked him for his guidance, and I did change.

> *The way of a fool is right in his own eyes, But a wise man is he who listens to counsel.*
> Proverbs 12:15

As the season progressed, instead of motivating and teaching the boys more about the game, the head coach would demean and belittle the players. The following are some "coaching strategies" he used. He would throw his hands in the air in disgust when a player struck out, and on one occasion I saw him throw his hat on the ground when errors occurred. I saw tears come into one child's eyes when he verbally abused him on the playing field about an error/mental mistake. During the first of the season, he told the players to take off their vest and hats and pile them up so he could wash the stink out of them. That was his way of telling the team they played a terrible game. After one particular game, he told the team some players may not be called to play again because certain boys did not play well or did not meet his expectations. This created tremendous anxiety for the players because they never knew if they would be called back. The boys just wanted to play ball, improve their skills, and have fun. The strategies this coach used caused the players to feel defeated and unsure of themselves. His philosophy was to bring about change in the team through fear. Jesus did not frighten children or nonbelievers in order to bring about change in their lives. Jesus should be our role model in every endeavor.

I noticed when we did not play for a weekend or two, the players would come back more relaxed and ready to play. As the tournament progressed, the head coach would become more critical of their performance. They seemed to become more tense and intimidated by him. They actually played worse in most cases as the weekend went by. During a game one of the infielders made two errors in one inning; the coach told the child that his errors were going to cost us the game. I could not understand why the coach did not encourage the player. Instead, he humiliated the player and harped on the consequences of those two mistakes. Remember this is youth league baseball. The player knew he misplayed the balls; he felt bad enough without the comment being added by the head coach. The child's dad told me about the comment the coach made to his son. His son would not say a word on the way home because he felt defeated by the coach.

As I tried to stand up for the boys, conditions worsened for my son. The coach was more insulting and ugly to my son when he made an error or struck out. The weekend prior to quitting the team my son made seven hits out of ten appearances at the plate; the two games we won that weekend, he drove in the winning runs. With a .489 average my son was batting 150 points higher than any player on the team except for one other player that joined the team later in the season. The next weekend when my son played, the coach told him the bat he was using was too heavy and to use a lighter bat. This was his regular bat. His tone to my son was very degrading. The batting coach was in disbelief that the head coach was so determined to make a bat change minutes before the game was to start. After the team left the batting cages and went to the field, I asked the coach why he would change his best hitter's bat. During our conversation he changed his stance on the bat and said my son could use it. After all the discussion about the bat, the coach placed Matt, one of his best hitters, last in the batting order. The bat issue was not over in the coach's mind. At the team meeting after the game, he told Matt not to bring the heavy bat back to his team. The tone of vengeance in his voice made my son cry. At the sight of this, the coach said to the team, "And we know who will go crying to his daddy." I know Jesus would not use vengeance like this toward anyone.

Instead of having a confrontation in front of the team, I waited to speak with him in the parking lot. He stated he had nothing to say to me or my wife. I realized at that point he was spiteful and did not have the knowledge or wisdom to discuss an issue with an open mind. How good of a coach could he be? He did not seem to be concerned about the well-being of my child or the other children. I realized that for him the game was not about the children; it was about him being in control and having absolute authority. He took revenge on my son because I questioned his coaching abilities and his negative behavior toward his players. I realized this man was out of control. Needless to say, my wife and I pulled our son off the team.

My human spirit initially wanted to show the head coach the error of his ways. The thoughts going through my mind were neither kind nor Christian. I was shaking with anger. If I did not have the Lord in my heart, this incident could have escalated to a fight or even worse. I had never seen an adult be so mean and spiteful to my son. Once I calmed down, I realized what I wanted to do to him would not accomplish anything. I prayed about it, and God sent my heart the answer. Since the coach would not talk with me, I decided to write him a letter while opening the door for him to call me and discuss our spiritual foundation, Jesus Christ. I hoped that if he saw how I felt, he would be open minded enough to talk with me. I realized I may not get a phone call from him, but this was the only way to handle the matter; it gave me peace once I dropped the letter in the mail to him.

I recall years ago someone telling me I needed to be open minded. I never really understood that comment until I faced reality—That is, until I faced God's love. God opens our minds and wakes our spirits to new things and new ways. If your old ways are not working, try something different. Now I understand it.

A gentle answer turns away wrath, But a harsh word stirs up anger.

Proverbs 15:1

*The wise in heart will be called discerning, And
sweetness of speech increases persuasiveness.*
Proverbs 16:21

I talked with a few parents of players that quit the team.
They stated they would avoid the head coach in the future
or ignore him if their paths crossed again. He had created
so much tension. Based on my direction from the Lord,
I had to try to share my Christian faith with him. I truly
feel by the way he treated parents and children he was not
walking with the Lord in his heart. His actions indicated
he has knowledge of the Lord only in his mind. By taking time to write him, am I judging him or am I trying to
counsel him by sharing the light of the Lord? I can only
try to share my experience with the Lord.

After we quit the team, I apologized to my son for
leaving him in that situation for so long. I got caught up
with the excitement of seeing my son play ball and tried
to find the positive areas present in this team. Just as I
was, parents were not concerned about the head coach's
attitude until it affected their children. I can understand
their reasoning because they wanted to see their children
play ball on a good team.

While playing other teams, I saw coaches screaming at
boys when they were losing. It was more than motivational
screaming in the excitement of the game; it was degrading. Some of our fans saw an assistant coach for another
team throw his son against the dugout fence; we could
hear the dad screaming at his son all the way out in right
field. The umpires did not take control of this disgusting

behavior and did not eject the coach from the game. On the other hand, I saw a more head coaches encouraging and showing their players how to correct their mistakes.

From the beginning of the season until the start of the next season, nine players left the coach's team. Some of the players only played a weekend while some finished the season. I do know the majority of the players did not come back to the team because their parents became disillusioned with the coaching philosophies and antics used by the head coach. Unfortunately, as players were leaving, more were in line to replace them.

The second team that Matt played for was a city league team that played during the week. Some of the boys on this team had never played organized baseball. The head coach was encouraging and supportive while delivering direct instruction. The players loved him and were not scared of him. When a player made errors or were not focused on the game or practice, he would show the player what they did wrong in a positive manner along with cracking jokes to get them refocused on the game.

It was exciting to see a player get his first hit in a game or make his first catch. Our team won the league's regular season championship and the season ending tournament. This unlikely group of boys developed into a winning team. This shows that a coach does not have to demean and belittle players in order to create a winning team. As parents, we have to demand coaches build and not destroy the confidence of young players. Listed below are a few positive strategies the coach used:

- He would ask a player what he did wrong on a certain play.

- He would explain why a play should have been played differently when a player made a mistake.

- He would try players at different positions to find out where they were best suited for their skills.

- He talked with individual players showing them their strengths and weaknesses.

- He encouraged his players to practice at home to improve their skills.

- He used the bench by letting a player sit out an inning or two to improve his attitude if a player was not hustling.

- He would go to the pitcher's mound and crack a joke to settle the player down if he was not throwing accurately. He gave the player a vote of confidence in their performance.

- He was direct in his expectations of the team. He expected the players to stay focused on the game.

- He showed positive reinforcement while showing patience when a player made an error.

This coach brought out the best in his players through positive instruction. He used godly principles. He put Biblical instructions into action. Through his actions this coach helped my son rediscover the joy of the game.

I mentioned that I probably would not get a response from the letter I sent the coach that we played for on the weekends. I was almost sure he would not call. I was wrong.

He did call. He immediately stated that I was a disgruntled parent because my son was not good enough to be a starter on his team anymore and would never be good enough to play high school ball. He went on to be critical of my wife and me. He was going in all directions, criticizing anything I might be remotely connected to. He went on to say a few things about his current team. They were winning without the players that quit; they were having fun without us. He also tossed a few more criticisms at me.

Basically, his objective for calling me was to criticize my family since he thought I was being critical of him. I had hoped for a different outcome. I feel his intention was to build himself up by making my family seem bad. He was trying to make himself feel better about the situation while thinking he got the best of me. The only thing I felt bad about was that he thought I was trying to judge him; I had no intention of doing so. There is only one judge, and that is God. I wanted to share my experiences with him in a humble conversation. God knows which spirit each of us is carrying. Our actions most of the time truly tells someone what spirit we are carrying in our hearts. During his conversation he did not mention Jesus or God.

I realized during the conversation that his words were being used for revenge. While he was rambling in our conversation, I thought of two other dads that had sons on the team and they experienced the same criticism of their family in a telephone call. He was consistent in his actions, and this was not an unusual occurrence. Jesus would not treat people in this manner. The truth is the truth; it will set us free from turmoil. I quickly realized this while ending the conversation.

> *But the fruit of the Spirit is love, joy, peace, patience, kindness, goodness, faithfulness, gentleness, self-control; against such things there is no law. Now those who belong to Christ Jesus have crucified the flesh with its passions and desires. If we live in by the Spirit, let us also walk by the Spirit.*
>
> Galatians 5:22–25

> *But prove yourselves doers of the word, and not merely hearers who delude themselves. For if anyone is a hearer of the word and not a doer, he is like a man who looks at his natural face in a mirror; for once he has looked at himself and gone away, he has immediately forgotten what kind of person he was. But one who looks intently at the perfect law, the law of liberty, and abides by it, not having become a forgetful hearer but an effectual doer, this man shall be blessed in what he does. If anyone thinks himself to be religious, and yet does not bridle his tongue but deceives his own heart, this man's religion is worthless.*
>
> James 2:22–26

Based on what that coach said, my family was a total failure. My human nature wanted to match criticism for criticism. If I had given into the temptation, I could have been very cruel; I did not let his comments bring me down to his level. God does not want us to retaliate with revenge. He wants us to show His love for everyone. Before I ended the conversation, I wished him and his team the best. I hope that he reflects on my actions, and it brings his awareness to another level. The coach crossed the line in the way he treated my son. It was my duty as a parent to stop this mistreatment. I will support my son in a positive way. Unfortunately, people like this coach will cross our paths whether we initiate the association or whether it is initiated by others. Their negativity and actions can bring us down quickly if we allow the interaction to continue. I feel this man is unaware of the consequences of his actions. He drives people away from him. I feel sorrow for him because of his unawareness. I have often hurt people or have made wrong decisions. I know people have felt sorrow for me. In this situation I tried my best to put on the Armor of Light in dealing with him.

> *The night is almost gone, and the day is at hand. Let us therefore lay aside the deeds of darkness and put on the armor of light.*
>
> Romans 13:12

> *Now flee from youthful lusts, and pursue righteousness, faith, love and peace, with those who call on the Lord with a pure heart. But refuse foolish and ignorant speculations, knowing they produce quarrels.*
>
> II Timothy 2:22–23

I often make mistakes and feel I do not deserve God's love and forgiveness. It is hard for me to share God's love with someone when I have feelings of inadequacy. We still need to share God's love with people. Everyone makes mistakes. Too often people enjoy seeing someone else make a mistake or fail. I wish I could have gotten to the point where the head coach and I could have talked about the Lord. I truly do not know where his faith lies. I do know his actions on the baseball field and his relationship with parents is not good. As a Christian, I do have a right to disagree with his actions and stand for what I believe, as he has the right to react to the stand that I take.

I learned a lot through this experience. I never thought if someone hurt my son I could act in a godly manner toward that person. With God in my life, I was able to share His attitude with the coach while we were on that team and afterwards. It was tough to be civil during this time, but I realized it was the only way to handle the situation. I will pray for him. I pray that if he is rough or is spiteful to a child that he feels the Lord convicting his heart. With time he can change. I can allow someone like this who has a pessimistic attitude to lead me, be a part of my life or I can walk away. As you know, my family chose to walk away.

> *You have heard that it was said, "An eye for an eye, and a tooth for a tooth. But I say to you, do not resist him who is evil; but whoever slaps you on the right cheek, turn to him the other also.*
> Matthew 5:38–39

Since I placed my son in a tough situation, we talked about the different coaching strategies the two coaches used. He said he was nervous when playing for the coach on the weekend because he never knew how he would be treated. He preferred the coaching strategies of his city league coach because it was fun. Matt's experiences playing on these two teams gave him a better understanding of the spirit of darkness and the spirit of lightness. He can clearly see that God expects us to be at peace with everyone and enjoying being with each other. I asked Matt which coach he would imitate if he ever became a coach. Of course, he said, "The fun coach." Our children do learn from their experiences, especially if we communicate with them. This means we have to ask the right questions and teach them. They learn from our actions and our attitudes. They learn from others. If we try to teach the Spirit of Light, we are giving them the best preparation for whatever comes their way.

During this time a dear friend of mine Ernie stated to me one day that God will sort us all out in the end. It brought a smile to my heart; I liked the concept of the word *sort*. In the end God will sort through the sanity and insanity that transpires in our lives. Hopefully we will all gain His sanity before our lives expire on earth.

I believe if you have the Spirit of the Lord in your heart, you realize you are not always right in your actions. You can recognize your mistakes quicker. It is then easier to a give a sincere apology to someone you hurt, misguide or say a cruel word. With the Lord in your heart you become a better person and will become a better leader. When people do not have the Spirit of the Lord in their heart, most of the time they feel they are always right. There is no reasoning with people like this. If you listen closely, their reasoning justifying their actions does not make sense at all. They tend to justify a wrong in any way they feel they can; it seems they dance around the truth because their hearts do not allow them to hear the truth.

I realized during this time that too many coaches and individuals use demeaning tactics to motivate someone to perform. I know Jesus would not use tactics like these. He would use positive motivational techniques. I encourage all parents and adults to stand up for our children. We must set good examples for our youth and teenagers. Positive motivational techniques can be used to hone skills and bring someone to gain self-confidence in his or her performance. Can you think of any ways to build up a person's self-confidence?

Individuals that oversee programs need to take complaints seriously and deal with pessimistic leaders quickly before they ruin our youths' outlook toward life. Too often valid complaints are ignored or not dealt with properly. Afterwards retaliation is taken out on our children. People do hold grudges. Many times individuals need to be removed as leaders since their pessimistic attitudes will not change, but for some reason or another, they are not.

When dealing with athletic competition, parents and coaches need to show control. When we divert to negative gestures such as screaming and loud demands, this shows we are out of control which will affect a player's performance. Many parents spend time coaching their children at home and even become a coach for their teams when the children are younger. I have done both. I had to learn not to be a coach from the sidelines when my son is playing for someone else. I realized my coaching from the sideline is a distraction to my son and the coach. I have also seen coaches that coach their own children place more demands on them and have greater expectations for them to perform. Their demands can become a distraction to other players on the team. When coaching or teaching our own children about life, our methods should not intimidate or defeat them.

You may wonder why I talked so much about my experiences on the baseball field. I had to apply many Biblical principles in dealing with the bad situation I was in. They are listed below:

- Self-Control, controlling anger and lashing out with abusive words
- Trying to be a disciple for the Lord
- Being able to forgive the coach
- Apologizing to my son
- Walking away from an abusive situation
- Teaching and asking my son the right questions so he could see how we should conduct ourselves
- Depending on the Lord for guidance

Unfortunately we can not always shelter our children from abusive actions and expect them to make the right decisions. They are individuals, and they will make mistakes. Hopefully, we can show them the right attitude they need to be successful. The attitude I am referring to is the Spirit of the Lord. Our children must learn to stand up for themselves, make the right decisions that affect their lives or others, and in order to have peace forgive people that hurt them. Sometimes, they must choose to disassociate from abusive people or people that could get them into trouble. We must learn to do the same for ourselves. We encourage our son to talk to us about issues and conflicts in his life. People can be cruel and unaware of their actions. I have. How about you? As parents we are trying to teach our son to treat people the way Jesus would, to be humble and kind. If others do not allow this and are mean to him, he needs to walk away from them. It is hard for a young one to grasp this concept. Even though I can grasp it, I struggle with staying calm when someone hurts me or my family!

Thoughts for Reflection

- As a Christian, we can stand up for what we believe. We should care for the person no matter what actions they have taken against us. We can offer our counsel while disagreeing with their actions. In the end we may have to separate ourselves from certain people.

- If we keep an open mind, we can learn from others. During the time my son was playing travel ball I did try to coach him from the sidelines because I did not want him to make any mistakes. I saw the consequences of mistakes made on the field. The coach did mention that I should not be coaching from the sidelines. I agreed with the coach and stopped. It is sad that the coach did not have an open mind to apply what I was trying to convey to him.

- The good baseball coach walks with the Lord in his life. He is a special person. We should show more appreciation and thanks to people that lead our youth in the ways of the Lord.

- We can allow people to defeat our spirit. Think of their ways as ignorant, smile to yourself, and know God loves you. I have allowed people to defeat me before I found God.

- Individuals with authority need to realize they can be a better leader using positive techniques versus being pessimistic.

- When we stand up for what is right we need to use the armor of God, His Words and His Spirit.

- A friend of mine told me I was wasting my time contacting the negative baseball coach. He had always acted like this, and he would not change. As a disciple of Christ, we must not give up on others. They may not change today, but our actions may bring them to a new awareness another day.

- You probably have heard the expression "misery loves company." Some people are so dysfunctional that the only way they can make themselves feel better is by trying to make others feel worse.

- Your actions speak much about the kind of person you are.

Bible Verses for Study

Then he taught me and said to me, "Let your heart hold fast my words; Keep my commandants and live; Acquire wisdom! Acquire understanding!

Do not forget, nor turn away from the words of
my mouth.

Proverbs 4:4–5

But I say to you who hear, love your enemies, do
good to those who hate you, bless those who curse
you, pray for those who mistreat you.

Luke 6:27–28

Now the deeds of the flesh are evident, which
are: immorality, impurity, sensuality, idolatry,
sorcery, enmities, strife, jealousy, outbursts of
anger, disputes, dissensions, fractions, envying,
drunkenness, carousing, and things like these, of
which I forewarn you just as I have forewarned
you that those who practice such things shall not
inherit the kingdom of God.

Galatians 5:19–21

But He gives a greater grace. Therefore it says,
God is opposed to the proud, but gives grace to
the humble."

James 4:6

I delight to do Thy will O my God; Thy Law is
within my heart.

Psalm 40:8

It is the Spirit who gives life; the flesh profits
nothing; the words that I have spoken to you are
spirit and are life.

John 6:63

And we urge you, brethren, admonish the unruly,
encourage the fainthearted, help the weak, be
patient with all men.

I Thessalonians 5:14

Questions

1. Can you think of a time that you could have shared the
    love of Jesus with someone, but have chosen not to make
    the effort? If the answer is yes, why did you not do so?

2. I do not like to confront someone because it is stressful.
    Could this be that we feel we have our own short com-
    ings and do not want to seem we are judging someone?

3. Who gives us wisdom in our lives?

4. Do your children or close friends feel comfortable con-
    fiding in you? What does that tell you about the spirit
    you portray to others?

5. How can you possess a humble spirit?

6. Is the head coach that demeans and hurts children with
    his words walking with the Lord, or is his spirit in limbo
    in this part of his life?

7. Which coach or type of personal behavior would you want influencing your children's life?

8. Why do so many people miss having a personal relationship with the Lord and walk in darkness all of their lives?

9. List a few ways how a positive attitude/drive can enable you to be more successful in accomplishing goals.

Supporting
Your Child

As parents, my wife and I hope that we will be able to teach and show our child about God and the way He wants us to live our lives. Through Jesus Christ, God gives us real life examples of how to create and maintain healthy relationships. We have spent hours teaching our son how Jesus wants us to treat others and how he should act in his young life. When Matt was in elementary school, the answers seemed to make sense to him, but as he faces adolescence the issues become more complicated. Questions surrounding relationships become more intense especially in the arena of dating. When I was entering this stage of life, my parents gave me a book to read. They told me to read it and ask them questions. I was too embarrassed and unsure what to ask, so I told them I did not have any questions. I always felt it was hard for me to talk with my parents about personal issues. Adolescent changes can be a very hard topic to discuss with a twelve-year old, but if parents do not jump in and take the lead, uninformed friends may try to fill in the gaps. I did spend time with my son talking about the changes in his life that were about to take place. My goal was to build a foundation, so he would feel like he could talk to us about any issue that comes up. I hope that as he hears his friends talking about some of the issues he will remember that we talked about them first and come to one of us for answers. It is often uncomfortable talking about intimate issues with our children, but they need to know we are ready and willing to discuss these things.

If the lines of communication are kept open, all involved should feel more comfortable discussing and sharing important thoughts and ideas. As Matt grows up and thinks about marriage, I hope my wife and I get the chance to know our future daughter-in-law, as well as her family. It is important for the families that will be joined together through marriage to support the couple. As in every stage of Matt's life, I will stress the importance of God's will and direction in the monumental decision of whom he wants to marry. I will talk to the young lady about her commitment to God and question how she sees God's role in their marriage. It is very important to have common beliefs and values for a marriage to have a chance to last—God's union. I will recommend Christian counseling before the decision to marry is made. I know from my personal experience it is impossible to make a marriage work without God at the center so I will stress the importance of a God-centered marriage. I will also be candid about problems that will arise even with God as the center and assure them that my wife and I will always be there for them if they encounter problems. If they encounter problems, that may cause them to think about divorce; I will work with them to find the resources needed to support their marriage Although I am not advocating anyone stay in an abusive or unsafe marriage, I do believe that couples often take the quick way out. I want Matt to know that a good relationship takes work and commitment even when it might feel simpler to just quit.

> *Where there is no guidance, the people fall, But in abundance of counselors there is victory.*
> Proverbs 11:14

> *Do not be bound together with unbelievers; for what partnership have righteousness and lawlessness, or what fellowship has light with darkness?*
> II Corinthians 6:14

Children need instruction about relationships, marriage, commitment, communication, finances and most of all, love. While it is important to discuss these issues, it is also important to model a godly approach to these subjects. My parents were married for fifty-three years, and although it was not a perfect marriage, the Lord gave them the determination to stay together.

When I decided to marry Pam, my parents voiced their concerns about the relationship, but I was not willing to listen. Once they saw that I was not going to heed their recommendation to halt the marriage, they gave up on trying to convince me. My parents knew that I was strong-willed and not open to hearing their ideas or following their guidance. If I had been open to hearing my parents, I could have learned from their life experiences. As parents, we must model godly relationships; hopefully some of our godly actions will be ingrained in our children's spirit. I believe that if I had followed the Lord as a young man, I would have seen that I was choosing someone that did not walk with truth or commitment. I now realize without the Lord as the foundation in my life the marriage was doomed to fail. The Bible verse from II Corinthians 6:14 clearly states that a relationship should not be unequally yoked.

> *Do not be bound together with unbelievers; for what partnership have righteousness and lawlessness, or what fellowship has light with darkness?*
>
> II Corinthians 6:14

In order to really know a person and understand them, we need to take into consideration his or her past home environment. When I met Pam, I should have talked to her about the Bible and God's will. I'm sorry I did not have the knowledge to ask God for insight and wisdom about my relationship with her. I was not depending on God. I was depending on my own judgment. More than anything I wish that I had found out if she had the love of Jesus in her heart before I gave her my heart. The Lord can be your counselor and guide. If we use our faith and take the time to listen to His guidance, He will direct us down the right path. We must believe, we must hear, and we must follow. Even when we do not follow His lead, the Lord can turn a negative situation into a positive one.

I pray that my son has God's spirit and wisdom to look at the whole person when he considers having a life partner in marriage. I hope the wisdom he gains in life will allow him to be aware of all aspects of their lives, including their spiritual foundation and how they handle their finances. Will that person be willing to work together with him to achieve common spiritual goals and commitments including those concerning finances? Spiritual differences and financial stresses in a marriage are often reasons for divorce.

As parents we must share our knowledge with our children. I want my son to trust God in real-life situations. It is my duty as a parent to teach him, guide him and counsel him, even when he is an adult.

Thoughts for Reflection

- We should not hesitate to give our children godly counsel and guidance even when they are adults.

- I wear a necklace with a cross as a reminder that Jesus died on the cross for me. Consider giving someone you love a necklace with a cross as a gift. This shows them you and Jesus loves them.

- Take time to observe life around you; slow down! You may find to your surprise that you enjoy seeing a beautiful sunset, kids playing, people interacting with each other, etc. This could give you peace and joy for a few moments and relieve the stress in your life. Enjoy your children at any age of their lives.

- Abuse can be physical or mental. Mental abuse can be very hurtful; from my perspective it is when we allow someone's actions or words to defeat us. We begin to doubt ourselves. We feel worthless in others' eyes and we lose our self-confidence. We should question if we should stay in a relationship with an abuser.

- I find myself being more critical of my actions when I make mistakes or when someone else makes me feel that I am at fault. I question what I could have done to have a more positive outcome. I dwell on my decisions or choices more than the turbulence others have created for me.

- Our children will be better off if they learn at a young age to depend on the Lord.

- Parents need to believe their children can be successful.

Bible Verses for Study

But if any of you lacks wisdom, let him ask of God, who gives to all men generously and without reproach, and it will be given to him.

James 1:5

The wisdom of the prudent is to understand his way, But the folly of fools is deceit.

Proverbs 14:8

For such is God, Our God forever and ever; He will guide us until death.

Psalm 48:14

Listen to counsel and accept discipline, That you may be wise the rest of your days.

Proverbs 19:20

Questions

1. Can our actions tell someone about our walk with the Lord? What actions are you revealing to others? Are you going through the motions with your walk with the Lord, or are you truly doing your best?

2. Why is it important to teach your children about God?

3. How can you teach and share with your children and others about the Lord?

4. Did you feel comfortable confiding with your parents? If not, why?

5. Was there ever a time when you looked back and regret not listening to your parents? If you had listened, how could it have changed your life?

6. If you did not teach the spiritual foundation about the Lord to your children, but accepted Him into your life years later after they were grown, have you shared with your children that you found the understanding about life? If not, why?

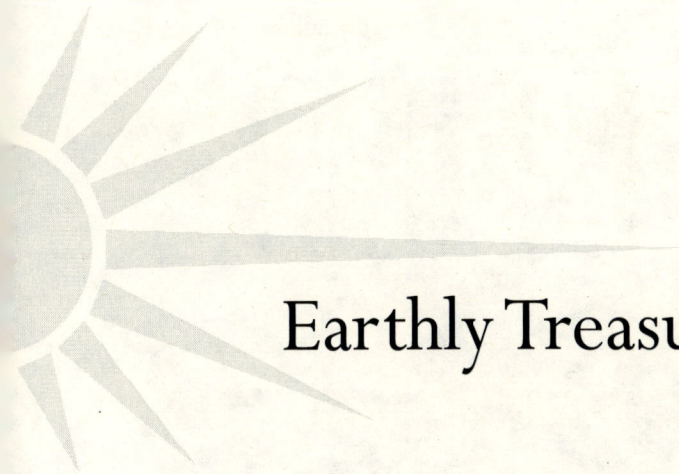

Earthly Treasures

There are many verses in the Bible that address wealth and money. I once heard that money is mentioned 2300 times in the Bible. God has a lot to say on the subject! I feel God wants us to work hard each day, to be blessed and to prosper. Yet, He does not want our main purpose in life to be the acquisition of riches. The key is how we acquire the wealth and what we do with the blessing. God does not want us to be overwhelmed with money issues, thus making money the most important thing in our lives. Money and finances affect us in all phases of our lives. I would like to share with you a few things I have learned over the years and things God has taught me about finances.

He who loves money will not be satisfied with money,
nor he who loves abundance with its income.

Ecclesiastes 5:10

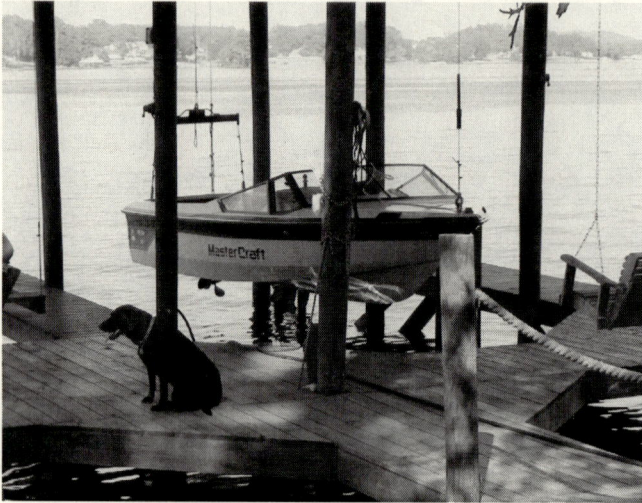

Why do Some People Have More Opportunity
and Acquire More Wealth than Others?

It is interesting how the Bible verse below states: "It is easier for a camel to go through the eye of a needle, than a rich man to enter the kingdom of God." I believe this statement was made because many people are driven to achieve a large amount of wealth. They spend all of their time and energy driving toward that goal and possibly hurting people in their paths. Money becomes their god and the true God takes second place. They spend no time experiencing our richest blessing, the grace of our Lord. Often we miss the Lord because we are focusing on other treasures. There are wealthy people that have a personal relationship with

God; they share their wealth and consider it a blessing to
do so. There are poor people that have a personal relationship with the Lord and share their blessing. No matter if
we are a poor man or a rich man, the only way to enter the
kingdom of God is to know God.

> *And Jesus said to His disciples, "Truly I say to you, it
> is hard for a rich man to enter the kingdom of heaven.
> And again I say to you, it is easier for a camel to go
> through the eye of a needle, than a rich man to enter
> the kingdom of God." And when the disciples heard
> this, they were very astonished and said, "Then who
> can be saved?" And looking upon them Jesus said to
> them, "With men this is impossible, but with God all
> things are possible."*
>
> Matthew 19:23–26

> *For where your treasure is, there will your heart be also.*
>
> Matthew 6:21

We have all seen or heard about individuals that take
advantage of older people through schemes that separate
them from their life savings. If you have older parents,
you need to take the time to watch out for their finances
before someone else does. It is also not unusual for family members to steal money from family. This destroys a
family unit. Unfortunately, this has happened in my own
family. Has this happened to your family?

> *Wealth obtained by fraud dwindles, But the one who
> gathers by labor increases it.*
>
> Proverbs 13:11

Over the years I have seen companies go out of business because their owners did not realize that dishonesty and poor quality of work would destroy their future. If you treat people with respect, are dependable, provide quality work while charging a reasonable price for your services, customers will request your business in the future. Happy customers will tell others about your business. Unfortunately some people do not realize this while taking advantage of others. They hurt themselves more than they realize.

We need to do our best in following God's commands in order to be successful.

A good name is to be more desired than great riches,
Favor is better than silver and gold.

Proverbs 22:1

You know the commandments, Do not murder, Do not
commit adultery, Do not steal, Do not bear false witness,
Do not defraud, Honor your Father and Mother.

Mark 10:19

Just as God directs other aspects of our lives, His word has information on how we should conduct ourselves in relation to debt. Credit card debt causes enormous stress on individuals and families while destroying financial security. Many file bankruptcy. Debts incurred should be paid off. A commitment to repay money loaned was made to the credit card company and, when it is due, it is the borrower's responsibility to repay it. If the discipline to pay off the cards each month is not there, then it is better not to have them. You need to have sufficient funds to pay off the balance monthly. Credit cards can be a blessing to use when you pay the balance off or they can be a curse if you are living beyond your means. Credit card companies prefer you not pay off the balance so they can charge you their high rate of interest. If you are not careful, the interest you pay for your original purchase can be many times what the item cost. In some cases if the balance gets to high, it may take years to pay off the balance even if you stop using the card. God's instruction concerning debt allows us to live a freer, more joyous life.

Credit cards make it too easy to have instant purchases; then all of a sudden you realize as the months have gone by that you have over spent buying furniture, items for the new apartment or new home, the big screen TV, the new refrigerator, all of the Christmas gifts, clothes, etc. It is a great feeling initially when we are able to purchase things on credit, but is it worth the temporary lift when we get the bill? Many of the purchases should and can wait until we have the cash in hand to pay for the merchandise. It has gotten to the point where we want immediate satisfaction with our purchases. We can't wait. The debt along with the high interest rates can destroy our future financial freedom. We need to use self-control in dealing with our finances, especially the use of credit cards.

> *But the fruit of the Spirit is love, joy, peace, patience, kindness, goodness, faithfulness, gentleness, self-control; against such things there is no law.*
> Galatians 5:23–24

My parents taught me that I needed to live within my financial means, while not acquiring a tremendous amount of debt. Along with God directing me, I was able not to burden myself with debt. As a result, I have not had a car payment since I was in my mid twenties, nor have I had to pay large amounts of interest on credit cards. I was thirty-eight years old when I made my last house payment. You can accomplish this payoff at a young age, too. This way of life has brought me financial peace. My philosophy is that when I make monthly payments for something, I am paying for someone's nice vacation or big salary when I could be investing the money toward my own financial future or tithing for God's work. Many people believe they are better off deducting the mortgage interest on their income taxes. In fact, they may only get one third of their money back, depending on their tax bracket.

Although God gives us clear direction about money, He also gives us the ability to use our mind. We must take responsibly when it comes to investing wisely. When I was younger I did not have the financial knowledge of investing money. I regret not seeking out Christian financial seminars to attend in order to learn more about stocks, bonds, and mutual funds, along with diversification of investments. We need to be able to trust our advisors, but we also need to learn enough to know what they are doing. Mutual funds are very popular investments today. You need to understand the differences between no-load, front-end load and back-end load funds. Be careful of additional fees being charged by brokerage firms. The fees can strip you of earnings while the firm makes a good profit for themselves. A few times over the years I have taken advice of my adviser when I knew I should have listened to my heart and bought various stocks while being advised not too. Sometimes the risk is worth the reward if you can afford to lose a small amount of money.

Often we do need to take steps in moderation. We need to begin saving for our future when we are young even if we can save only small amounts. We cannot depend on government obligations or retirement promises to take care of us during retirement. Do not hesitate to ask God for guidance in financial matters. He will give you peace and guidance. The parable of the Talents below represents resources and gifts we are given. God gives us the gifts and resources to use in all aspects of our lives including money. If we do not use them in a Biblical manner then we do not get the most out of our lives.

> For it is just like a man about to go on a journey, who called his own slaves, and entrusted his possessions to them. And to one he gave five talents, to another, two and another. one, each according to his own ability; and he went on his journey. Immediately the one who had received the five talents went and traded with them, and gained five more talents. In the same manner the one who had received the two talents gained two more. But he who received the one talent went away and dug in the ground, and hid his master's money. Now after a long time the master of those slaves came and settled accounts with them. And the one who received the five talents came up and brought five more talents, saying, Master, you entrusted five talents to me; see, I have

gained five more talents. His master said well done, good and faithful slave; you were faithful with a few things, I will put you in charge of many things; enter into the joy of your master. The one also who had received the two talents came up and said, Master, you entrusted to me two talents; see, I have gained two more talents. His master said well done, good and faithful slave; you were faithful with a few things, I will put you in charge of many things; enter into the joy of your master. And the one also who had received the one talent came up came up and said, Master, I knew you to be a hard man, reaping where you did not sow, and gathering where you scattered no seed. And I was afraid, and went away and hid your talent in the ground; see, you have what is yours. But his master answered and said to him, You wicked, lazy slave, you knew that I reap where I did not sow, and gather where I scattered no seed. Then you ought to have put my money in the bank, and on my arrival I would have received my money back with interest. Therefore take away the talent from, him and give it to the one who has ten talents. For to everyone who has shall more be given, and he shall have an abundance; but from the one who does not have, even what he does have shall be taken away. And cast out the worthless salve into the outer darkness; in that place there shall be weeping and gnashing of teeth.

Matthew 25:14–30

When you get out on your own, you will have a house payment or rent and maybe a car payment. You can survive without credit card debt if you live within your means. You can save on expenses in various ways. Listed below are a few things I have done over the years:

- Take your lunch to work instead of eating out.

- Rent a movie and watch it at home instead of going to the movies.

- Cook a good meal at home instead of eating out which could include having friends over and letting them bring a covered dish.

- Learn to complete a home project yourself instead of paying someone to do the work.

- Go to the park and play tennis.

- If friends or family have a nice get-away place, take advantage of visiting them instead of going on an expensive vacation.

- If you are single, you can share the expenses of an apartment or house with a friend.

Theses are a few ways that you can save money while not spending excessively. Can you think of more ways to save expenses and still enjoy life? Can you think of necessary debt that you need to live and think of unnecessary debt that you can do without?

Is Your Spiritual or Financial Life a Wreck?

Today with the turmoil in our financial service sector with defaults on mortgages and other various loans. It is sad because so many people are being impacted by losing their homes, jobs and investments in the stock market. We are facing the worst recession in decades. Many call this the greatest recession since the 1930s. Blame for this recession can be placed on agencies that oversee lending practices and/or the greed of banks and mortgage companies wanting to make gobs of money on loans, as well as individuals borrowing money without using common sense. Greed has affected individuals that have saved and invested for their futures in the stock market. This destruction happens when the stock market declines rapidly because of fear. In this major downturn, many have seen their lifesavings dissipate while having to change their lifestyles drastically to survive. During this time we have witnessed one of the largest Ponzi schemes in history where an estimated $50 billion was bilked from investors by one trusted individual.

A Ponzi scheme is a fraud in which early investors are paid off with funds raised from later ones. Many charities and individuals have lost everything due to this fraud. Everyone gets hurt by people borrowing beyond their means and individuals living off others through fraud.

To help get our economy out of this recession, a scheme called a stimulus package worth almost a trillion dollars to create jobs and get money flowing back into our economy for fixing the financial mess was passed by Congress. Unfortunately more money is being borrowed by our federal government. Many disagree with this move because of the cost of the added debt. Do you think the stimulus package should have been passed? Living beyond our financial means can lead to destruction and to misery. This should be a wake up call about how harmful too much debt can disrupt one's life.

> *And there were others who said, "We are mortgaging our fields, our vineyards, and our houses that we might get grain because of famine." Also there were those who said, "We have borrowed money for the king's tax on our fields and our vineyards. And now our flesh is like the flesh of our brothers, our children like their children. Yet behold we are forcing our sons and our daughters to be slaves, and some of our daughters are forced into bondage already, and we are helpless because our fields and vineyards belong to others."*
>
> Nehemiah 5:3–5

I am concerned about the way our government is being run. Our government is not using any practical sense in controlling debt. Unfortunately our government has created trillions of dollars of debt for us by overspending and not using our tax dollars wisely. A good example of this debt is our social security program. Money paid into the system that was not needed for social security benefits at the time was spent on other needs. The excess money should have been set aside for Social Security and invested properly. There is a projected shortfall of taxes being paid into the program. My concern led me to write the Social Security office about the soundness of our program. Their reply was: "The law requires that taxes like social security be placed in the general funds of the Treasury then distributed to a few various trust funds. The law allows that assets not needed for current benefits and administrative expenses be invested in interest-bearing obligations of the United States. Special obligations must pay interest equal to the prevailing rate on outstanding Federal securities. The securities held by the trust funds consist of short-term certificates of indebtedness and longer term bonds. They are called special issues because they are issued only to Social Security trust funds. The special issues are not the same as T-Bills and Treasury notes because they are available on the open market. Special issues are not. In order to repay the borrowed money the Government will need to raise money as it does for all other needs, through an increase in general tax revenue or by increasing borrowing from its the public."

Our government does not follow the same accounting rules that they require businesses to follow. I am amazed how law can allow spending the excess money from our social security taxes for other needs. I am fearful our government's debt will one day place us in a great recession or depression. What would happen if a program like social security could not meet the obligations to the elderly? This shows a tremendous amount of debt is not good.

Change can affect us in many phases of our life. Often we do not have control of things that transpire. I would like to show you how change has affected me and my family in one phase of our lives. Often changes in regulations are driven by lobbyists while our elected officials vote for the changes with no regard as to how it will impact people. While working with a large corporation, my retirement benefits were drastically reduced because regulations were changed to give companies the flexibility to reduce retirement benefits. From my perspective the changes in retirement compensation allowed corporate leaders to benefit financially while promises to the middle and lower level workers were broken. During this time corporate leaders in upper management gained much higher compensation packages by reducing future retirement benefits to their employees. With less payout to retirees, the top leaders of a company could show a higher profit margin to their shareholders or just shift the money to themselves. In turn they have been rewarded with higher compensation packages. Often the CEO of a company making the decision to reduce retirement benefits simply justified the reduction by saying other companies are doing so, and so can we because this is the trend. The change in regulation has affected millions of people. I personally lost seventy percent of my retirement benefits that were promised to me when I began working with the corporate company. Our lawmakers should not be allowed to make these changes, but they do. If they do make changes like this, the reduction in benefits should also apply to them. There are too many double standards in this country. Too often life seems not to be fair. Commitments and promises made should be kept. Are they broken for the love of money - greed? Below *The Parable of the Rich Man and Lazarus* will make all of us think about greed and eternity.

Now there was a certain rich man, and he habitually dressed in purple and fine linen, gaily living in splendor every day. And a certain poor man named Lazarus was laid at his gate, covered with sores, and longing to be feed with crumbs which were falling from the rich mans table; besides, even the dogs were coming and licking his sores. Now it came about the poor man died and he carried away by the angels to Abraham's bosom; and the rich man also died and was buried. And in Hades he lifted up his eyes, being in torment, and saw Abraham far away and Lazarus in his bosom. And he cried out and said, Father Abraham, have mercy on me and send Lazarus, that he may dip the tip of his finger in water and cool off my tongue for I am in agony in this flame. But Abraham said, Child remember that during your life you received your good things and likewise Lazarus bad things, but now he is being comforted here and you are in agony. And besides all this, between us and you there is a great chasm fixed, in order that those who wish to come over from here to you may not be able and that none may cross over from there to us. And he said, Then I beg you Father that you send him to my father's house for I have five brothers that he may warn them, lest they also come to this place of torment. But Abraham said, They have Moses and the Prophets; let them hear them. But he said, No, Father Abraham, but if someone goes to them from the dead, they will repent! But he said to him, If they do not listen to Moses and the Prophets neither will they be persuaded if someone rises from the dead.

Luke 16:19–31

As a parent it is my responsibility to teach my child about finances and share what I have learned over the years. God wants us to give our children guidance in all phases of their lives. I want to teach my son about spending money wisely and saving for his future. I am going to make the effort to share the knowledge that I have learned over the years about finances with my son. I plan to set up an investment account in both our names when he gets older. He'll be able to watch ten different stocks over a few years, and I will help him learn how to make decisions about when to sell or keep a stock based on its performance. He is already learning how to build equity into a home, and I hope to teach him how to assess good real estate investments. While teaching Matt about money, I also want to model and to stress the importance of developing a good work ethic, treating people with respect and honesty.

Has buying material things lead you to financial ruin? Are you spending your money wisely? Is it sinful if overspending is due to pride, envy, or gluttony? Have you purchased an expensive car because your neighbors or friends have one? Could you have purchased a more economical vehicle? Have

you joined a country club because it makes you feel important? Do you buy things on sale even if you do not need
them? Do you blame others for your debt? I have often heard
people say that credit card companies are to blame for their
debt. We have to take responsibility for our actions. Have
you ever blamed your spouse for your financial troubles? Do
you constantly go to sales and buy things you really don't
need because there was a good price on the item? Do you feel
you cannot control your spending? God has the answers. I
make the time to pray about making a big purchase. If I have
peace in my heart, I will proceed with purchasing the item.

> *The rich rules over the poor, And the borrower becomes
> the lender's slave.*
>
> Proverbs 22:7

We are responsible for our actions. Discipline is required
in all phases of our lives. Companies use advertising to
convince us to buy the latest and greatest products immediately whether it is the big screen TV or newest model
car. Look around; is your house filled with clutter and purchases that you really do not need or use? Material things
do not make us happy. At the time, when we are making
our purchases, it is so easy to justify our spending until we
get the bills in the mail. Then we get that sick, sinking
feeling. If you feel like you need to make a purchase, go
to God. He may show us that we do not need the item.
When thinking about buying an item, we just need to ask
ourselves do we really need it and can the purchase wait.
Often if we wait, the item may go on sale later.

We can justify our spending in many ways. One way we justify the things we buy for our children is by telling ourselves that these purchases are okay because we do not want them to feel deprived. We want them to have more than we did. We often place too much importance on buying too many things for our children. I am the world's worst. One of my weaknesses is I try to buy my son all the sporting equipment I think he needs! Sometimes we just need to let our children be creative. When I was growing up, if I did not have a skate board, I would make one out of an old pair of roller skates and a piece of wood. It was fun being creative. I had great fun making and playing with my homemade toys. What causes you to buy things that you really do not need? Are your closets packed full, your garage or basement filled to capacity? If so, you may need to take time to realize you may have a spending problem and deal with the issue.

Most of us have a conscience and can feel God directing us. We often do not listen to Him. Is carrying the guilt in your heart worth it when taking advantage of someone in order to gain financially? Is living from paycheck to paycheck worth the toll it takes on your peace of mind? What happens when you lose a job or you are out of work due to sickness and you have a tremendous amount of debt? Other issues with having debt are that we cannot save for the future nor have funds set aside in case of unexpected expenses. Money issues create added stress on our-selves, our marriages and our families. The key is whether we are single or married; our goal should be to acquire financial peace. God wants us to handle our money wisely and not be wasteful. We need more self-control in all phases of our lives. God does not want us burdened with a tremendous amount of debt. God wants us to be content in our lives.

Thoughts for Reflection

- Our decisions or non-decisions in life can affect us for years to come.

- To keep our sanity we need to depend on the Lord for self-control in our lives.

- Keep your focus on the Lord. He will bless you.

- Debt adds stress to our lives. Strive for the minimum amount of debt possible.

- You can have financial peace if your finances are in order.

- Our relationships are more important than accumulation of vast amounts of money.

- Often we need to be content where we are in life, not striving for more.

- To be successful, we need God in all aspects of our lives.

- We can justify any action or decision we make. Sometimes a *trend* can be used in the place of stating it is *greed* that resulted in the decision. Which word is inclined to make us feel it is okay to justify our actions?

- Difficult times force us to change.

- God does want us to help the less fortunate.

- Our earthly treasures can be taken away due to

sickness, loss of a job, a bad decision, and surely at death.

Bible Verses for Study

"Do not lay up for yourselves treasures upon earth, where moth and rust destroy, and where thieves break in and steal. "But lay up for yourselves treasures in heaven, where neither moths nor rust destroys, and where thieves do not break in or steal; for where your treasure is, there will your heart be also.

Matthew 6:19–21

Not that I speak from want; for I have learned to be content in whatever circumstances I am.

Philippians 4:11

For wisdom is protection just as money is protection. But the advantage of knowledge is that wisdom preserves the lives of its possessors.

Ecclesiastes 7:12

Behold, I am coming quickly, and My reward is with Me, to render to every man according to what he has done.

Revelations 22:12

Then your heart becomes proud, and you forget the Lord your God who brought you out from the land of Egypt, out of the house of slavery. "Otherwise, you may say in your heart, 'My power and the strength of my hand made me this wealth.' "And it shall come about if you ever forget the

Lord your God, and go after other gods and serve them and worship them, I testify against you today that you shall surely perish. "Like the nations that the Lord makes to perish before you, so you shall perish; because you would not listen to the voice of the Lord your God.

Deuteronomy 8:14,17,19–20

Then the Lord spoke to Moses saying, "When a person sins and acts unfaithfully against the Lord, and deceives his companion in regard to a deposit or a security entrusted to him, or through robbery, or if he has extorted from the companion, or has found what was lost and lied about it and sworn falsely, so that he sins in regard to any one of the things a man may do; then it shall be, when he sins and becomes guilty, that he shall restore what he took by robbery, or what he got by extortion, or the deposit which was entrusted to him, or the lost thing he found.

Leviticus 6:1–4

He who tills his land will have plenty of food, But he who follows empty pursuits will have poverty in plenty.

Proverbs 28:19

He who is gracious to a poor man lends to the Lord, And He will repay him for his good deed.

Proverbs 19:17

He who shuts his ear to the cry of the poor, Will also cry himself and not be answered.

Proverbs 21:13

Behold, we are slaves today, And as to the land which Thou didst give to our fathers to eat of its fruit and its bounty, behold we are slaves on it. And its abundant produce is for the kings Whom Thou hast set over us because of our sins; They rule over our bodies And over our cattle as they please, So we are in great distress.

Nehemiah 9:36–37

And He said to them, "Beware, and be on your guard against every form of greed; for not even when one has abundance does his life consist of his possessions."

Luke 12:15

Questions

1. Did your parents teach you about financial matters as you were growing up?

2. Why is it harder for a rich man to make it to heaven?

3. Can a person be financially prosperous, laden with a tremendous amount of debt?

4. How can instant credit like a credit card destroy personal finances?

5. What does God say about having too much debt?

6. Why are some people blessed with more wealth than others?

7. List five ways to decrease monthly expenditures to save for the future.

8. Why does God want us to be content in our circumstances?

Wisdom

When I was in a state of desperation trying to find the truth about life, God led me to study the books of Proverbs and Ecclesiastes. If you are searching for wisdom and purpose, I encourage you to read both books. The assumed writer Solomon was a leader and a teacher relying on his personal experiences to show us the best way to be fulfilled in life is to follow and love God. Through his writings he hoped future generations would be spared the pain of learning the hard way. He hoped people would not have to go through life apart from God. Solomon wanted people to have a fruitful life at a young age instead of having to experience failure after failure. His writings provide us direction to live a good and successful life. When Solomon became king, he asked God for wisdom; God blessed him with his request. Solomon became the wisest man in the eastern world. The hardest part for me is to take what I read, follow the advice, and truly live each moment for God. I hope you embrace Solomon's wisdom and have God at your side.

> *And Solomon's wisdom surpassed the wisdom of all sons of the east and all the wisdom of Egypt.*
>
> I Kings 4:30

> *Therefore, since we have so great a cloud of witnesses surrounding us. Let us also lay aside every encumbrance, and the sin which so easily entangles us, and let us run with endurance the race that is set before us, fixing our eyes on Jesus, the author and perfecter of faith, who for the joy set before Him endured the cross, despising the shame, and has sat down at the right hand of the throne of God. For consider Him who has endured such hostility by sinners against Himself, so that you may not grow weary and lose heart. You have not yet resisted to the point of shedding blood in your striving against sin.*
>
> Hebrews 12:1–4

The book of Proverbs is great to begin teaching our youth about wisdom. The first nine chapters speak directly to them. One of our main missions in life as parents is to teach our children about the Bible and God. I feel if we try to teach them about wisdom at a young age, they may be spared the pain of learning many life lessons the hard way. Listed below are a few themes[5] of the book that will enlighten everyone's spirit.

Wisdom God wants us to be wise. He portrays two paths people take. The first path people take is when they are foolish, stubborn, wicked, and ignorant. The second path people take is when they seek to know and love God with all their heart.

Relationships God gives us direction in developing relationships with others. These relationships are with friends, co-workers, strangers, and family members. In all relationships we must show understanding, moral standards, and most importantly love.

Work God wants us to work hard and not be lazy. We must be diligent and have discipline to complete tasks. We must provide for our families along with helping others when we can.

Speech How we talk reflects what we are really like. It shows our real attitude toward others and ourselves. Our speech shows people how wise we have become. Do we have a foul mouth (cursing), skirt around the truth (lie), etc? Do we speak the truth, show compassion and have love for others in our words? Do we speak of Jesus or mention God?

Success

Too often we work hard for money and fame. We place our success on how much material wealth we have accumulated. God views us as being successful when we have a good name, have moral character, are devoted to following Him, and share His love with others through being disciples. All our resources, time, and talents come from God—be thankful to Him.

It is interesting how Proverbs touches on success. The definition of *success*[6] is satisfactory completion of something, the gaining of wealth and fame. For many years I placed so much emphasis on the material things I could acquire. I worked hard and I was driven to save for my future retirement. I came to the realization that I really do not know what is in store for me tomorrow, and I need to focus more on today. I placed too much importance on material things and hard work. The Lord made me realize that I need to enjoy the things He has already given me. I need to find a balance in my life of hard work, the drive to save for the future, and building relationships. He has shown me I should be working harder on relationships with others. I still have much work to do toward building relationships. Without the Lord in my life, I had a big empty spot in my heart. My heart was missing the love of our Lord. I often feel I do not deserve God's grace because of my actions.

Many times in our lives we are so focused on self-satisfaction along with acquiring wealth and fame, we lose perspective of right and wrong. We are driven to accomplish our goals while God is overshadowed in our lives. When God is placed in the background, we tend not to be completely satisfied in anything we do; we are always striving for something different. God commands us to place Him first in our lives. With His direction we can find satisfaction and contentment. There is no doubt in my mind that God wants us to be successful by working hard and He wants us to have the things we need. We should have Him as our top priority in life, walking in His ways. Through this I realized I can have many successes in a day. For me the best success I can have in a day is being kind to others. Most importantly, when I reach heaven, I hope I will have achieved the successes the Lord had planned for me. Success begins with knowing God and His direction for us.

The book of Ecclesiastes teaches that wisdom begins by seeing life from a divine perspective and trusting God. Without this knowledge our efforts are futile, and we lack purpose of life on earth. Only God can provide our ultimate satisfaction, joy, and wisdom. By the way, the book is only twelve chapters long. If we could absorb all of the knowledge and wisdom in this book alone, we could live a most rewarding life. Listed below are a few themes[7] of the book that may lead you to read Ecclesiastes.

Searching   We search for satisfaction and test the world for happiness. We cannot find enjoyment, meaning, fulfillment, happiness without God in our lives.

Emptiness	The pursuit of worldly pleasure, wealth, and success is disappointing. Our hearts will be empty and restless in our pursuits.
Work	There is no lasting reward in hard work without God as the basis for living.
Death	In the end God will judge each person's life. Human achievements are futile while godly achievements are everlasting.
Wisdom	Human wisdom and education have their limits. In order to understand life, we need the guidance and wisdom found in God's words. God's words are found in the Bible.

The words *vanity* and *futile* are used frequently in the book of Ecclesiastes; the definition of vanity[8] "is something that is vain, empty, futile or useless." In Ecclesiastes, Solomon takes us on his life journey explaining how everything he tried and tested was an exercise of futility. Solomon had it all from a worldly perspective. He had wealth, power and knowledge. Near the end of his life, he looked back with an attitude of humility and realized most things he had done in his life were meaningless and empty when he was apart from God. Solomon filled this book with his practical and spiritual wisdom for everyone seeking the truth about life.

Proverbs and Ecclesiastes both contain guidance on wisdom. Wisdom is one of the most powerful possessions we can obtain as an individual. One of the greatest lessons I learned from reading these books years ago was that they contrasted life with and life without wisdom. Life with wisdom leads us to make good decisions. Life without wisdom leads us to make poor decisions. Following God's wisdom is the best course to minimize hurt, grief, and misfortune. The sooner we learn this, the better off we will be. Wisdom involves having diligence and discipline in our lives; unfortunately, discipline has been an issue in some phases of my life. I have too often had to learn the hard way, from my mistakes.

I feel wisdom is a gift from God, and if we use this gift, we can learn a lot about a person if we truly listen when they speak. The other night on television I saw an interview with a well-known CEO who had been retired from his company for several years. During the interview, he discussed how difficult it was for him to lay off his employees when the business went into a decline. He stated he cared about his employees and talked about other aspects of business. Then the host of the show asked him what was the most difficult question he had ever been asked. The CEO said that he was once asked whether he thought he would go to heaven when he died. His response was he thought he would even though he had been divorced twice. He was basically a good person, a hard worker, and treated people the way he expected to be treated. During the interview I was waiting for him to include in his response words such as by the grace of God or "by my acceptance of Jesus Christ I know I will have eternal life in heaven." He never stated this. It seemed he was still struggling with the answer. I realize that some people have a hard time expressing themselves about religion and eternity. It is a difficult question to answer. We must carry the faith, show grace, and thank God for allowing Jesus to die on the cross for our sins.

> *For by grace you have been saved through faith; and that not of yourselves, it is the gift of God; not as a result of works, that no one should boast. For we are His workmanship, created in Christ Jesus for good works, which God prepared beforehand, that we should walk in them.*
>
> Ephesians 2:8–10

That same man and his current wife had recently written a book together about being successful and how to become a winner in business management. He travels around the country as a motivational speaker at business seminars. People attend his seminars because they want to follow in his footsteps. He is a highly regarded figure in the business circle due to his innovative management strategies and leadership style. Many people say when it comes to speaking about business, he is dynamic and innovative. During this time I could not help but think how he would impact people's lives if he could speak as strongly about Jesus Christ and God.

Often we strive to be winners on earth by gaining riches and working all of the time while being apart from God. What will matter in the end is if we are a winner in God's eyes. God gives us understanding about life. God can give us insight to listen to someone's speech. Next time truly listen to someone speak. Afterwards ask your-self, "What did I learn about that person?"

He who loves purity of heart and whose speech is gracious, the king is his friend.

Proverbs 22:11

Years ago in my younger days before I found God, I had a foul mouth–I used a few choice curse words. After I found the Lord, He showed me how ignorant I was and how thoughtless the words sounded when they came out of my mouth. It did not take long for me to stop saying them. I was amazed how humbled I became when I acci-dently used one of the words! This shows you the Lord can change someone's spirit.

Either make the tree good, and its fruit good; or make the tree bad, and its fruit bad; for the tree is known by its fruit. You brood of vipers, how can you, being evil, speak what is good? For the mouth speaks out of that which fills the heart.

Matthew 12:33–34

Prayer for Realization

For this reason, I bow my knees before the Father, from whom every family in heaven and on earth derives its name, that he would grant you, according to the riches of His glory, to be strengthened with power through His Spirit in the inner man; so that Christ may dwell in your hearts through faith; and that you, being rooted and grounded in love, may be able to comprehend with all the saints what is the breadth and length and height and depth, and to know the love of Christ which surpasses knowledge, that you may be filled up to all the fullness of God. Now to Him who is able to do exceeding abundantly beyond all that we ask or think, according to the power that works within us, to Him be the glory in church and in Christ Jesus to all generations forever and ever. Amen.

Ephesians 3:14–21

Where Will You Finish in the Race of Life?
In the Light or In Darkness

Thoughts for Reflection

- We deprive ourselves of good things by not knowing God and His direction for us.

- Even with the Lord in our lives, we make mistakes; we are not perfect once we accept the Lord's grace and His love. I wish I could be perfect like Jesus. Often my mistakes hurt myself or others.

- Never take each other for granted. Show your love and appreciation in some way every day. Tomorrow may not be in our destiny.

- Your words and actions should be the truth, not lies. People will love you the way you are.

- You can have spiritual peace and contentment if your life is right with God.

- Many times we realize we have an issue in our lives that we need to correct. So often we do not make the correction because change is difficult. Change can make each of us a better person.

- Be content where you are in your life today. Enjoy the day. God can get you to the point of laughing at most of your silly mistakes. Life can be fun and does not have to be taken so seriously.

- Through our faith, God does give us hope for a better day.

- Be kind, courteous, and caring toward all people. This will come back to you as a blessing.

- With wisdom comes knowledge.

Bible Verses for Study

A wise man is cautious and turns away from evil,
But a fool is arrogant and careless.

Proverbs 14:16

And to know the Love of Christ which surpasses

knowledge, that you may be filled up to all fullness of God.

Ephesians 3:19

The fear of the Lord is the beginning of wisdom, And the knowledge of the Holy One is understanding.

Proverbs 9:10

He presented another parable to them, saying, "The kingdom of heaven is like a mustard seed, which man took and sowed in his field; and this is smaller than all other seeds; but when it is full grown, it is larger than the garden plants, and becomes a tree, so that The Birds of the Air come and Nest in its Branches.

Matthew 13:31–32

I can do all things through Christ who strengthens me.

Philippians 4:1

Man in his pomp, yet without understanding, Is like the beasts that perish.

Psalm 49:20

Hatred stirs up strife, But love covers all transgressions.

Proverbs 10:12

My son, if you will receive my sayings, And treasure my commandments within you, Make your ear attentive to wisdom, Incline your heart to understanding; For if you cry for discernment, Lift your voice for understanding; If you seek her silver, And search for her as for hidden treasures; Then you will discern the fear of the Lord. And discover the knowledge of God. For the Lord gives wisdom; From His mouth come knowledge and understanding. He stores up sound wisdom for the upright; He is a shield to those who walk in integrity, Guarding the paths of justice, And He preserves the way of His godly ones. Then you will discern righteousness and justice And equity and every good course. For wisdom will enter your heart, And knowledge will be pleasant to your soul;

Proverbs 2:1–10

And you were dead in your trespasses and sins, in which you formerly walked according to the course of this world, according to the prince of the power of the air, of the spirit that is now working in the sons of disobedience. Among them we too all formerly lived in the lusts of our flesh, indulging the desires of the flesh and of the mind, and were by nature children of wrath, even as the rest. But, God being rich in mercy, because of His great love with which He loved us, even when we were dead in our transgressions, made us alive together with Christ by grace you have been saved,

Ephesians 2:1–5

For the one who sows to his own flesh shall from the flesh reap corruption, but the one who sows to the Spirit shall from the Spirit reap eternal life.

Galatians 6:8

But I say, walk by the Spirit, and you will not carry out the desire of the flesh.

Galatians 5:16

Questions

1. What was Solomon's purpose for writing the book of Proverbs?

2. What was Solomon's purpose for writing Ecclesiastes?

3. Solomon was considered the wisest man of his time. Why?

4. Why is it hard for us to take lessons from the Bible and apply them to our lives?

5. How do you reconcile the world's idea of success and God's plan for success?

6. Why is it important for us to teach our children and our youth about God?

7. How can our attitude and behavior affect what we accomplish in life?

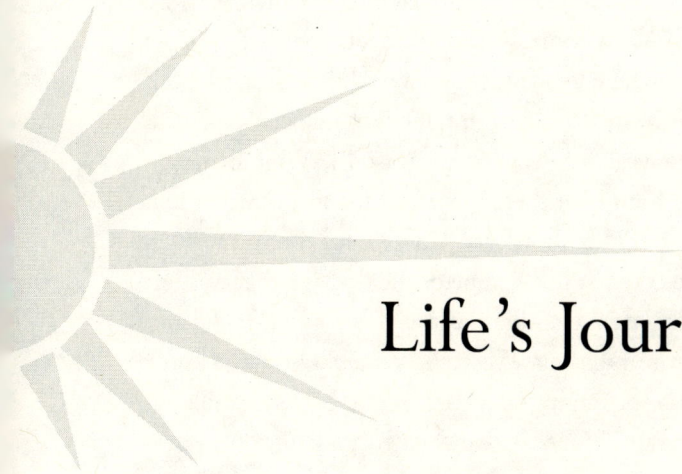

Life's Journey

Placing your faith in the Bible is not easy for many people because Jesus is not tangible in an earthly way. One cannot physically touch or see Him, yet I know Jesus is real, and the Bible is the truth. I had Jesus standing in front of me, and He called me His disciple. Even so, it took me years to acknowledge Him. I had to go through a difficult time in my life to finally get it—what I was missing in my life and that He was truly there for me. Since I found Jesus over twenty years ago, I have made many mistakes. I have gained wisdom through prayer, reading the Bible, and experiencing life. God has helped me to understand life and the reasons why people act or react the way they do. I would like to share my experiences and thoughts that have brought me to this place in my life.

My Choice

After the first few years of marriage to my first wife, we decided to build a home. We bought a lot on the Mississippi Gulf Coast where we worked. I realized that since we built the house one-half mile from the ocean, the consequences could be grave during hurricane seasons. While living on the coast, I found out there was about ten feet of water that surged inland when hurricane Camille hit the coast. Even though we could still see some of the damage that was left fifteen years after Camille destroyed the coast, it did not deter us from building. We could possibly lose our home and all of our belongings if a hurricane as big as Camille hit the coast again. However, we decided that since we knew the history, we would build the house on piling twelve feet in the air to prevent as much water damage as possible if water surged inland. We acquired flood insurance just in case a hurricane flooded the house or knocked it down.

I had never experienced a hurricane or a divorce before I located to the Gulf Coast. Divorce was not something I had ever thought about, so I did not know the extent of the damage it could cause to my life and home. I did; however, realize the destruction a hurricane could cause. When we divorced, our "home" was destroyed even though our "house" was not. I led myself to this destruction because our marriage was not built on God's foundation. Soon after I divorced, I left the area to work in another region of the country. About fifteen years later, before I left my corporate job, my territory changed, and I covered the Mississippi Gulf Coast along with other southeastern states.

After hurricane Katrina occurred, I went to see the damage on the coast and also to see what happened to my first home. It was complete devastation. It was heart-breaking to see towns and communities destroyed. Lives were in total devastation from the massive storm surge. It looked like twenty-eight to thirty feet of water had surged over the area where I built my first home. The house was destroyed; it looked like the wood frame house had been lifted off the pilings and floated away like a boat.

Has Your Home Been Destroyed by a
Natural Disaster or by Divorce?

There were no signs of the house anywhere near the home site. As I drove down the road where the house had been, I noticed two churches within a quarter of a mile of my old home site. The churches were heavily damaged. The frame of one was still standing while the steeple of the other church was left lying on the ground. It was quite humbling to see the destruction of the area. I was overwhelmed that God's houses were right down the road from my old home, but I never attended church or stopped to thank God for what I had. I thought I had a good life, but now I realize that life can only be real and true through a personal relationship with Jesus Christ. I found this out during my separation and divorce. We are faced with choices all through our lives. I found out during that difficult time that I would need a spiritual foundation in order to rebuild my life. I would have endured less pain if I had made this decision when I was younger and had allowed Jesus to lead me. I personally believe God only wants the best for His children. We need to reflect inward and make a choice to have the Lord guide us before making major decisions.

> *Unless the Lord builds the house, They labor in vain who build it; Unless the Lord guards the city, The watchman keeps awake in vain.*
>
> Psalm 127:1

> *The Lord is near to the brokenhearted, and saves those who are crushed in spirit.*
>
> Psalm 34:18

The Lord teaches us in the Bible that we have a choice to *build our life and home on sand or on the rock foundation.* You have a choice to make if you do not yet know the Lord. Do you want to walk alone through life with no one to rely on or to give you the strength to weather bad times?

Jesus Christ is there to support all of us. He can teach you how to lead a life of success. When you speak to Him, open a Bible and read it while asking for His guidance.

Our Dreams and Gifts

I realized that since I did not have a relationship with Jesus at a young age, I missed out on many blessings. I tried to lead my own life and got caught up in worldly things. Meaningless issues brought me down. I was not using the gifts God gave me. Although I was a talented athlete, I applied myself only half the time. I sometimes wonder what would have happened if I had dedicated myself one hundred percent to be the best. Don't waste your talents. Stay focused on your dreams and be blessed by walking with the Lord. Do not let people's negativity and your mistakes get you down. Ask God for forgiveness and pray for the people that hurt you. There are many changes I still need to make in my life. Can you list any changes you would like to make in your life?

As I reflect on high school, I see that I should have been more focused on academics. Even though I only gave athletics a half-hearted effort, I gave academics even less. Perhaps I missed finding one of God's gifts because I did not apply myself when given the opportunity. God gives us all many opportunities to find and use the gifts He has given us. Even when we miss the chances God provides, He continues to give us other opportunities. I never thought I would have the opportunity to write a book, but God has led me to write His story in my life.

God gives us more than we can imagine, even more than we could ask for. He always wants the best for His children. This should and does motivate me to do my best at whatever God puts in my path today.

> *Whatever your hand finds to do, verily, do it with all your might; for there is no activity or planning or wisdom in Sheol where you are going. I again saw under the sun that the race is not to the swift, and the battle is not to the warriors, and neither is bread to the wise, nor wealth to the discerning, nor favor to men of ability; for time and chance overtake them all.*
>
> Ecclesiastes 9:10–11

While trying to motivate children in sports, we need to place more emphasis on life lessons and our spiritual foundation. Below are a few terms I heard coaches say when I played ball. As I reflect on these times I realize they were using these words to help us accomplish more in the sports we played. I encourage anyone leading our youth to take time to teach about life, not just sports or other activities. I did not apply all these principles off the field.

- Teamwork–Learn about relationships, supporting each other, joint effort, and working together.

- Perseverance–Have determination to complete the task or challenge ahead.

- Sportsmanship–Play fairly, be gracious whether you win or lose.

- Value of Hard Work–Learn to use your gifts God has given you to become better.

- Dealing with Adversity–You will not win all of the time. You will make mistakes. You will get more chances to succeed; make the next play. Don't give up or get down.

I realized these principles can be applied to more aspects of life. Below are examples of how the principals taught on the field can be changed to be used in the classroom, the work place and more universally into life. Can you think of other ways to use these principals in your life?

- Teamwork–Teachers and students work together in the classroom.

- Perseverance–Students are determined to pass and graduate.

- Sportsmanship–Students makes his or her grades honestly. Teachers and students show each other respect and courtesy.

- Value of Hard Work–Students are open to learning, they apply themselves and good grades are the reward.

- Dealing with Adversity–You will not always make the grades you desire. You are not perfect. You will get another chance to make a better score on the next assignment or test.

- Teamwork–Employees work together to accomplish goals in their work place set by the company.

- Perseverance–Employees are determined to have a successful company even when economic conditions change.

- Sportsmanship–Employees respect other co-workers

- Value of Hard Work–Employees work hard to become top performers so they and the company will be successful.

- Dealing with Adversity–Employees face adversity with a good outlook whether the company is going through layoffs, experiencing budget cuts, passed over for a promotion, have a difficult boss, etc.

I was an assistant coach on the baseball team of my son's favorite coach, whom I previously mentioned. Before each game we had a sports devotional focused on life and sports. We were able to teach about perseverance and adversity on several occasions. One lesson focused on the analogy of making mistakes on the field and in life. On the field, mistakes are called errors, but in life they are called sin. In athletic competition, as in the Christian faith, the chance to start over again is a gift. In sports we have the opportunity to make a better play next time, while in life we have the opportunity to make the right decision next time. God is forgiving. The key is we need to learn from our mistakes and do our best. We need to stay focused on what is ahead of us and not dwell on our past mistakes.

Do Not Give Up

Since I am a sports enthusiast, I have heard professional athletes talk about retiring when they get older, incurring injuries, no longer having the opportunity to prove themselves on the field, or not wishing to continue in the game. Some times these athletes simply give up while others decide to stick with the game. Some of the ones that stuck it out ended up accomplishing great things. They became part of a team that made it to the World Series or Super Bowl. Some even found opportunities to be mentors to younger players. My point in all this is "*Do not give up.*" If you do give up too soon, you may miss out on a blessing that God has in store for you. Continue to pray asking God's will. He will let you know when it is time to change directions.

When I was growing up and learning about life, I often felt discouraged about issues I faced. It seemed I had all of these thoughts and frustrations in my mind; I felt I had no one to share them with. I had a difficult time talking and sharing issues with my parents. Since I did not have God in my life, the isolation I felt was even greater. Even with support at home, children can be overwhelmed by things that are going on at school, things such as a break-up with a boyfriend or with a girlfriend, uncertainty of their direction in life, not knowing where they belong, what the future may bring them, the confusion of being hurt, or the divorce of their mom and dad. The list is endless. It is terrible when one parent disassociates himself or herself from their children. Children in this situation need to realize it is not their fault that the parent is acting in such a manner. Our youth and teenagers need to realize quickly that many issues like these are only temporary and are not meant to destroy their lives, but can actually make their spirit stronger. When I was younger, I tended to allow circumstances to get me down. If you are in a bad situation, try to keep a positive attitude while staying focused on the blessings you have. We often count the problems, dwell on each issue, but forget to praise God for the good things in our lives. Finding God's gifts and using them can bring us a tremendous joy, no matter our circumstances. I encourage you to be the best you can be; that is what God wants for all of us. Don't look back years down the road and say to yourself, "*I wasted so much energy on worldly hurt and worries.*" Overcome this now and apply your gifts. As parents we must focus on our children's spiritual development and help them understand life's lessons whether they are good or bad.

After I finished writing this story, I knew I needed an editor to bring the story to the level it should be since I am not a professional writer. I started to send copies and outlines of the story to publishers, an evangelist, and professional writers that friends knew. I received rejection after rejection. The two professional writers did, however, respond. One stated the story would never be published, and the other stated there were very few stories out there this bold; his feedback gave me hope. I prayed to the Lord that if He wanted it published, and if He wanted more people to see the story, I needed His help to find a publisher. I knew in my heart He wanted me to write it, and He directed me along the way in writing it. I began sharing copies of the story with co-workers, friends, acquaintances and even strangers. I was trying to be a disciple for the Lord. Everyone has a great story in life to tell, but I felt the Lord wanted me to share my story with more people. I was content to share His story as I was doing.

As time went by, I realized it had been over two years since I had the majority of the book finished; during this time I was adding bits and pieces to it. My Sunday school class, neighbors, and friends gave me hope that motivated me to keep working on the book. I knew in my heart the Lord wanted me to write it. I knew the story was to be shared with more people. This gave me hope, and I was not going to give up on the story and place it on the shelf to become covered with dust. Each day I hoped the book would get to the right person and become real; that is, become a published book.

For years I have thought of my wife as being the one in our family as having the strongest faith. While we were talking about the book one day, she stated that the Lord has helped the book make me a better person while maybe this was His plan all along. Over the few years, she had seen the disappointment I received when the bigger publishers responded with rejection letters. I found out that it is hard to get someone to publish your book if you are an unknown author and an unknown person. I am both. I thought to myself, *if only I was a known person.* I told Kelly that I still could not give up on the book going to print, and that I was still going to try to submit the manuscript to other publishers.

One morning I spent hours on the internet looking for Christian editors that could help me submit my manuscript to publishers or even publishers that would be interested in reviewing the manuscript. I found Tate Publishing Company that would be willing to review unknown authors' manuscripts. I had peace about sending the manuscript to them, but also due to all of the other rejection letters, I was apprehensive about their reply. They requested when I sent the manuscript to them to enclose a self- addressed envelope with enough postage so they could send the manuscript back to me. I only sent a self- addressed envelope with enough postage to cover a response for a letter not the manuscript. One day I noticed that a small package was at the front door. To my surprise it was from Tate Publishing. The package looked like it contained my manuscript, and I thought to myself it was nice of them to send it back, but it was not necessary to do so. To my greater surprise, it had a contract and a positive cover letter stating they were willing to publish the book. During the time I was reading the letter, I cried tears of joy, excitement, and relief. I stopped to thank God for this blessing. Tate Publishing Company is not a large publisher, but one day they could be by helping the Lord share His stories throughout the world. While these few moments were taking place in my life, my faith was reaffirmed that God does work in our lives if we follow His lead. Good things can happen to us in His timing.

Sharing God Love

We must share God and our lives with our children in order for them to see the Lord. Sharing God's love extends beyond this life. Nothing we give or buy for our children will impact their lives here on earth or eternity more than God's love. We need to be bold in Christ and be more open about what Jesus has done in our lives. Be a disciple for your children and others in the world. I want my child to have a life better than mine, with fewer mistakes. I want Matt to grow up listening to the Lord speak to his heart. A few years ago we gave Matt a chain with a cross so he could remember what Jesus Christ did for him. When he was playing his second season of baseball I encouraged him when he goes up to bat, to touch the cross and ask Jesus to help him do his best. My goal is to teach him at a young age to depend on the Lord in any situation. God wants the best for His children.

God speaks to us many times in the Bible on the subject of discipline. As parents we want to shelter our children from all the bad things in the world. This desire in itself is not bad, but when we do not allow our children to feel the consequences of their poor choices we do them a disservice. We may want to bail out our children in order for them not to feel the cost of their actions. God wants us to do the right thing and when we do not, He wants us to repent. But repenting does not mean we do not face the consequences of our choices. As parents we need to be consistent and diligent in teaching discipleship to our children. If we do not teach our children this principle, they will face many hard times and lessons as they mature. I am sure that no parent wants his or her child to make the same mistakes that he or she did. Godly discipline prepares children for the world. God disciplines us as His children; therefore, as parents we should disciple thorough love as modeled by Christ.

And you have forgotten the exhortation which is addressed to you as sons, "My son do not regard lightly the discipline of the Lord, nor faint when you are reproved by him; for those whom the Lord loves He disciplines, and He scourges every son whom He receives. It is for discipline that you endure; God deals with you as with sons; for what son is there whom his father does not discipline? Furthermore, we had earthly fathers to discipline us, and we respected them; shall we not much rather be subject to the Father of spirits, and live? All discipline for the moment seems not to be joyful, but sorrowful; yet to those who have been trained by it, afterwards it yields the peaceful fruit of righteousness.

Hebrews 12:5–7, 9, 11

One must be careful when being critical of a loved one. In my first marriage, I felt like I could not do even the smallest task correctly in the eyes of my spouse. Even washing dishes was a time for discouragement. My wife would inspect the dishes and throw up her arms saying that she would have to redo them since I didn't do them right. With criticism and no encouragement, I began to feel inferior and incapable of doing anything right. I allowed these bad feelings to exist in my life. It would have been more productive for her to say, "Honey, thank you for trying to help me, but you do need to do a better job." I allowed her cutting remarks to bring me down to almost nothing over the few years I was with her. I should have not allowed this to happen. Do not lose respect and confidence in yourself. My confidence today has been restored and I owe it all to my relationship with God. Your mind is powerful; God is powerful. Build others up; do not try to destroy them with your words. The sooner you realize you are special in God's eyes, the less you will allow others to defeat you.

Talking with people about the death of a spouse and/ or even losing one through a divorce is very hard. Death is the ultimate finality; there are no more chances to say, "I love you," or "I'm sorry." I've made the decision to make every day count with those dear to me because I do not know when the Lord will call them or me home. It was imperative for me to depend on God during my divorce because I thought I didn't want to live anymore. My life was based on an earthly person loving me, not God. Often we feel this way when a love one departs from us in death or divorce. Through this adverse time in my life, the Lord brought people into my life to show me how to strengthen my faith. He gave me understanding about life, but most importantly He gave me His love. Depend on the Lord first, not yourself or others.

A friend sent me an email sharing a testimony of a father that was asked to address a special House Judiciary Committee's subcommittee concerning the loss of his daughter in a high school shooting rampage. What he said to our national leaders was painfully truthful. They were not prepared for what he was to say, nor was it received well. Many times when a tragedy occurs, people tend to look for a reason why it happened and even try to place blame on someone or something. Politicians placed blame on our gun laws while thinking about placing more restrictive measures on guns. Restrictive laws can contribute to eroding away our personal and private liberties. It was inspiring when the father talked about the makeup of men and women who are three-part beings. We all consist of body, mind, and spirit. When we refuse to acknowledge our spirit in a godly manner, we create a void that allows evil, prejudice, and hatred to rush in and wreak havoc. The guns did not cause the death of the school children and teacher, but it was the spirit of the boys that planned and committed the massacre. What has happened to us as a nation? We have refused to honor God, and in so doing, we open the doors to hatred and violence. He went on to discuss how our heritage has been stripped away by restrictive laws such as not allowing prayer in our schools. This means we cannot openly talk of God in schools.

I agree that our laws are helping to erode and destroy our country. We have politicians that are creating laws who do not carry the spirit of God in their hearts. I believe with the Lord in our lives, we can make better decisions and are more open to listen to others. It is hard to be in the limelight of the public as an elected official since character flaws are brought to the forefront. None of us is perfect. Even with God in our lives, it is sometimes tough to make the right decision. What is happening to our nation as a whole? Are our values being lost?

Often when someone shares Bible verses with me that are special to him or her, I will write their name beside the verses to remember who shared them with me. When I was rebuilding my life spiritually, a friend of mine, Deanne, shared the verses below with me when I was lacking hope and strength. I often think of this scripture when I see a beautiful hawk flying in the air. I thank the Lord for giving me strength to carry on. We don't have any eagles flying around my part of the country!

> *Do you not know? Have you not heard? The everlasting God, the Lord, the Creator of the ends of the earth does not become weary or tired. His understanding is inscrutable. He gives strength to the weary, and to him who lacks might He increases power. Though youths grow weary and tired, and vigorous young men stumble badly, yet those who wait for the Lord will gain strength; they will mount up with wings like eagles, they will run and not get tired, they will walk and not become weary.*
>
> Isaiah 40:28–31

Focus

Many times we find ourselves questioning God as to why He has allowed so many bad things to happen in the world or to us personally. He does not make them happen. People who are not in a relationship with God make them happen or when we know God, we do not listen to Him. Our poor decisions, without the help of our Lord, make them happen. People who deny God make them happen. Therefore, it is our strength through Him and our faith that will change our lives. It is God's will for us to be compassionate, ethical, and follow Him. It is our human nature to ask *Why* when something bad has happened to us. We would be better off asking, *"What should I do next, Lord?"* instead of dwelling on something we probably cannot change.

I have chosen the love of Jesus Christ and eternal life. When I did not have the Lord in my life, I felt as through I was always missing something. I know Jesus Christ is real because He has come to me, and I have seen Him. If you are unsure which way to live your life, focus on what Jesus did on the cross for us and pray this prayer: *Please, Lord, bless my life with Your love, with Your peace, with Your joy, with Your understanding of life, and with Your wisdom. Lord, I cannot make my way in life without depending on You. I give my heart to You.*

> *Whoever denies the Son does not have the Father; the one who confesses the Son has the Father also.*
>
> I John 2:23

Staying focused on the Lord leads us to have a life of contentment, direction, and joy. It was hard for me to realize this until I experienced the love of our Lord. Place His love in your heart. Read your Bible daily and ask the Lord for His guidance. It is a peaceful and secure feeling to talk and pray each day to our heavenly Father. I often pray that I integrate into my life the things I learn in Sunday school, church, and Scripture. Life is a learning experience if we open our hearts to hear and see the truth about life. Our knowledge about life can be enlightened each day if we are open to listen to God. With knowledge, our journey in life becomes more complete.

> *Let no one look down on your youthfulness, but rather in speech, conduct, love faith and purity, show yourself an example of those who believe.*
>
> I Timothy 4:12

Listen to your heart because God is talking to you. Follow through with what He tells you so that you don't miss out on a blessing. I continue to learn from God and others. When I get to the gates of heaven, I do not want to have missed out on the many blessings the Lord wanted me to have. I have missed out on too many as it is. Perhaps you can understand because you feel there is something missing in your life. He showed me that I was not focused on Him each day, and I was not receiving His blessings to the fullest. I was failing to walk with Him daily.

When Jesus reminded me that I needed to share my story, which is His, it was a wake up call that I had lost my enthusiasm and excitement for Him. It felt like a train hitting me when he got my attention. While writing this story, I remembered the picture of Jesus that I received after my mom and dad died. I kept the picture and placed it away in a closet for years. It was the same picture that was hanging in the den that stormy night when Jesus appeared to me. I took it out of the closet, dusted it off, and placed it in my home where my family can see it every day. When I look at the picture, it is a reminder for me to stay focused on Jesus every day.

> *To sum up, let all be harmonious, sympathetic, brotherly, kindhearted, and humble in spirit; not returning evil for evil, or insult for insult, but giving a blessing instead; for you were called for the very purpose that you might inherit a blessing.*
> I Peter 3:8–9

I often hear people say that life is tough and hard. When I hear a comment like that, I think to myself - *In many instances we do make our lives difficult.* Every time I make an important decision without the benefit of the Lord's advice, I create a larger obstacle. My plans are often not what God has planned for me. I would make better, less complicated decisions with the Lord as part of my every-day life. Attending church and listening with an open heart is an amazing, uplifting experience. You will find yourself leaving the house of God with so much more in your heart than that with which you entered. I never thought I would say this, but church should always be a part of our lives. It is important to attend and grow with the Lord. I have noticed that my life is much better when I follow God's direction instead of my own. Being involved in church and with other Christians helps keep my focus on the Lord.

God wants us to stay focused on Him. Often we get too busy during the week and are exhausted by week's end. We often miss quality time with our Lord during the week. Sunday is a day for worshipping and rest. With worship comes refocus on what should be the most important part of our lives–God. We need support and love from other Christians. Having a church home and fellowship with others makes our lives more complete.

We who had sweet fellowship together, Walked in the house of God in the throng.

Psalm 55:14

*It is Important to Have a Church Home–I like
the Beauty of an Old Country Church*

Our minister is preaching this summer about prayer. He shared a story about "Just Pray" in our weekly church bulletin. Why is prayer often viewed as a last resort? We tend not to pray unless we are desperate, and by then, of course, we are. Why not pray when we first see the challenge ahead of us so that a small course correction will be all that is needed. An early correction would have put us right on target. Why wait? I hear people say that they don't really know how to pray. We get all concerned about saying the right thing to God, about not wanting to be selfish, and about not wanting to monopolize God's time, as if God were too busy to listen to us.

This story illustrates the absurdity of waiting for the right time or being in the right posture to pray. Three ministers were talking about the appropriate and effective positions for prayer. As they were talking, a telephone repairman was working on the phone system in the background. One minister shared he felt the key was in the hands. He always held his hands together and pointed them upward as a form of symbolic worship. The second suggested that real prayer was conducted on your knees. The third suggested that they both had it wrong; the position worth its salt was to pray while stretched out flat on your face. By this time the phone man couldn't stay out of it any longer. He injected, "I found the most powerful prayer I ever made was while I was dangling upside down by my heels from a power pole, suspended forty feet above the ground." Friend could it be that your best prayer just might be, "Help!" or perhaps, "Lord, I desperately need you right now." Let's lay aside our misplaced priorities and our feeble excuses and just pray.

After reading the article I thought to myself that often I pray for an answer. I get the answer. Then I ignore His directions. I want to follow my own plan. During this reflection I realized I seem to be too busy to take time to pray seriously several times a day. In my prayer time, I need to ask God to teach me to listen to Him and not waiver in His direction. Since I am not perfect, I realized that I have a few things I wanted to get under control in my life so I decided to work on one minor issue and focus on it through daily prayer. With God's help and by focusing on the issue in prayer, I am overcoming something that has been dragging my spirit down for years. Prayer does work. If we can overcome one small issue in our lives through prayer then we can begin building confidence in ourselves to accomplish other things in our lives.

While listening to a sermon in church the other day, I realized our minister was teaching from the Old Testament. Over the years I have found it difficult to spend much time reading some of the Old Testament scripture because it seems more complicated than the New Testament. As I sat listening, our preacher taught us that before Jesus gave His blood on the cross for our sins, animal blood sacrifices were used to atone for sin. The need for these sacrifices disappeared when Jesus died for us on the cross. Animal sacrifices were no longer needed because Jesus made the ultimate sacrifice. I know that God takes sin seriously. He gave his only Son for the sins of the world. Committing a sin hurts us, in our spirits and our bodies. It is not God's desire for us to make mistakes. While Jesus walked on this earth, He taught the truth of God's love for us and His expectation of us to love others. Once I accepted and understood what Jesus gave us when He died on the cross, I realized that I had been walking blindly in life and not realizing the true path my life should be taking. I knew undeniably that I needed to have the Lord as part of my life. He gave His life for me.

> *I acknowledged my sin to Thee, And my iniquity I did not hide; I said, "I will confess my transgressions to the Lord"; And Thou didst forgive the guilt of my sin.*
>
> Psalm 32:5

> *And one of the criminals who were hanged there was hurling abuse at Him, saying, "Are you not the Christ? Save Yourself and us!" But the other answered, and rebuking him said, "Do you not even fear God, since you are under the same sentence of condemnation? "And we indeed justly, for we are receiving what we deserve for our deeds; but this man has done nothing wrong." And he was saying, "Jesus, remember me when You come in Your kingdom!" And He said to him, "Truly I say to you, today you shall be with Me in Paradise."*
>
> Luke 23:39–43

One Sunday our minister's sermon addressed being in a rut. I felt as though our minister was talking directly to me. This often happens because the Lord is trying to get my attention. It takes an effort to get out of a rut or situation even if you do not like the circumstance. Change is tough because many times we become comfortable in our lifestyles; the unknown is scary to us. I quickly came up with a list of things that I needed to work on in my own life. When I was younger, I would rather have been anywhere else but in church. As I grow with the Lord and get older, I look forward to attending. I truly miss church when I am not able to attend. I find myself learning more about life and the Lord as I listen to the sermons and fellowshipped with others. That is why it is important to attend church.

In some churches, the clergy will not marry a couple without first spending time counseling them. That should be the normal course of action in all churches. This would be one way to learn where your potential partner stands with the Lord. Realistically you should know this before you even think about marriage with another! The priest or minister during counseling will ask direct questions about how you came to have a personal relationship with Jesus. He may have you share your favorite Bible verses. Then he will share with them what he has learned about them from these sessions. If necessary, he will explain why it is imperative that they have a godly union. He will also assure the couple the church is always there for them when problems arise. He may also offer the couple a book that they can keep at home to refer to from time to time. The couple, then, has the information needed to decide whether they are a good match and should marry. In preparation of my first marriage, we did meet with the minister for about an hour. He asked us about our faith in general, but not in detail. If he would have requested that I give him a few of my favorite Bible verses, I would have been dumbfounded to come up with any. The minister would have known I was not ready for marriage. I sometimes think in a case like this if ministers demand more time to counsel and guide couples before they commit to marriage, youngsters would realize there is more to marriage than just walking down the aisle and saying I do.

Over the years more ministers are requiring premarital counseling before they will perform a marriage ceremony, while some are even refusing to marry a Christian and an unbeliever. Premarital counseling should be a prerequisite to marriage to prepare a couple for what is ahead and why the commitment in marriage is so important. When making a lifetime commitment to someone, you definitely need to focus on knowing the other person's beliefs and values. You need to know that you are beginning your marriage with the Lord as the foundation of your home.

If you recall, when I was going through separation and divorce, I found our marriage license. It stated when we are united in marriage we become one with God. How can we become untied with God when God is not at the forefront of our lives?

Relationships

We would be very lonely if we did not have friends, love ones, acquaintances and marriage partners in our lives. Sometimes relationships seem challenging, complicated, confusing, and difficult. Over the years I have heard a statement that before you can have a meaningful relationship, you must love yourself first. I have to agree with this statement. God commands us to love our neighbors like ourselves. God is love. I realized before I accepted God's love I always felt I really did not like myself–love myself for who I was. Through His love I have gotten to the point where I like myself for who I am. When God is not first in our lives, we carry so much brokenness in our hearts due to our life choices–sin. We often hide our guilt, grief, and shame (iniquities) within our souls which often leads us to mistrust others. With all this doubt within us, we doubt others. We can challenge and bring turmoil in our relationships with others by not being honest and having a solid foundation with our Lord.

> *If, however, you are fulfilling the royal law, according to the Scripture, "You shall love your neighbor as yourself," you are doing well.*
>
> James 2:8

God wants us to enjoy life with others. God does not want us to cause hurt, confusion and discord in others' lives. When I find myself in a difficult situation with someone, I often want to act in the manner they are acting or worse. I have to take a step back and take a deep breath while asking Jesus how to handle the situation. If I listen to Him, He gives me understanding of the situation; He allows me to forgive the ones with whom I am in discord while showing leniency. Unfortunately, many times He shows me that the person is not walking in the light; he or she is unaware of their actions, and I should pray for that person. Sometimes He shows me that I am not right, and I can change for the better by dealing with the situation. By asking for God's help and His direction, I am able to work through the situation.

> *For Judgment will be merciless to one who has shown no mercy; mercy triumphs over judgment.*
>
> James 2:13

If God is in the forefront of our lives at a young age, He intends for us to abstain from sexual relationships until we marry. Why does He want this? The reason is that past experiences will haunt a new marriage. Since God is pure, He wants our marriage to begin untainted. For years the white wedding dress was typically used as a symbol for virginity. Over time the wedding dress has lost the connotation of virginity and is merely associated with a new bride. Would it not be great if we had self-control while following God's direction for us! Our lives would have more meaning and purpose. Sin causes conflict within our souls.

> For this is the will of God, your sanctification; that is, that you abstain from sexual immorality; that each of you know how to possess his own vessel in sanctification and honor, not in lustful passion, like the Gentiles who do not know God.
>
> I Thessalonians 4:3–5

The pain of deception and hurt by another in divorce does not always disappear after remarriage. I went through a period of time when I was responsible for putting stress on my marriage to Kelly. She knew something was wrong and was extremely patient with me. God had planned for us to be together. Together, the three of us, God, Kelly, and I talked about the struggles I was having with my previous marriage and the hurt I was still feeling. As a result, with understanding and patience, our marriage became better than ever. Communication between spouses is essential. Without it, one becomes distanced from the other and small issues become large issues that are damaging to the union.

The lack of intimacy between a man and wife is a major cause of affairs. Married couples need to communicate, and spend time with each other to feel close. We need to feel we are needed in each other's life. Too often we allow things going on in our lives to distance ourselves from each other. Without intimacy for a long time, frustration builds and often thoughts of extramarital affairs emerge. Most married couples will remember that intimacy was never a problem when they were dating or for the first year or two of their marriage. That's understandable since they weren't sharing a life together with all its responsibilities. All they had to think about were good times and when they would see each other again. Lack of intimacy is the biggest threat to a relationship. Satan is in the background cheering on the excuse to have an affair. Satan likes destruction, he loves to see marriages and families fall apart.

Adultery is wrong. Before going out and doing something that will change many lives, talk to your spouse about the issues pushing you in that direction. If necessary, see a counselor. Pray to God and ask Him to show you ways to resolves the issues. Often we know what the problem is, but it is hard to address the issue alone. Share your life with your loved ones; do not hold back. Ask your spouse to pray with you. Divorce should not be an option. Carry the Lord's grace in your heart, not Satan's desire to destroy and create selfishness. The Bible verses below make me tremble when I think of judgment day and then gives me hope. Everyone should have it engraved in his or her heart when dealing with others.

Anyone who has set aside the Law of Moses dies without mercy on the testimony of two or three witnesses. How much severer punishment do you think he will deserve who has trampled under foot the Son of God, and has regarded as unclean the blood of the covenant by which he was sanctified, and has insulted the Spirit of Grace? For we know Him who said, "Vengeance is Mine, I will repay," And again, "The Lord Will Judge His People."

Hebrews 10:28–30

To open their eyes so that they may turn from darkness to light and from dominion of Satan to God, in order that they may receive forgiveness of sins and inheritance among those who have been sanctified by faith in Me.

Acts 26:18

Today there is so much controversy surrounding homosexuality. There are legal fights in our court rooms trying to determine if same sex marriages should become legal. Some states are allowing this unity to take place, while others are ruling against it. I mentioned early in the book that I had a friend from work that was gay. I did not hold any hard feelings toward him, and I did not chastise him about his lifestyle. I feel God clearly states this is an unnatural act which is sinful. I feel God does want us to share with someone living this lifestyle that it is wrong and God still loves them. Often our minds allow us to justify our actions as being right because it makes us feel better. But do we really feel better by doing something wrong? God hates the sin, but loves the sinner. I cannot look down on someone that is a sinner because I am a sinner myself.

> *Therefore God gave them over in the lusts of their hearts to impurity, that their bodies might be dishonored among them. For they exchanged the truth of God for a lie, and worshiped and served the creature rather than the Creator, who is blessed forever. Amen. For this reason God gave them over degrading passions; for their women exchanged the natural function for that which is unnatural, and the same way also the men abandoned the natural function of the woman and buried in their desire toward one another, men with men committing indecent acts and receiving in their own persons the due penalty of their error.*
>
> Romans 1:24–27

I realize that I should be investing more of my time in relationships instead of projects around the house. I spent eights years of my life outside of my full-time job building my homes. I love to work with my hands, and I strive to complete projects. Trying to achieve a balance in my life is still a struggle. With a change of heart, I hope to build more meaningful relationships with others instead of working all of the time.

Eternity

God is disappointed that people break commitments and lie to each other, and that families are broken up through divorce. His children are abused on earth when they should be shown the love of Jesus. If you reflect on your life with Jesus, He will show you that we are nothing more than beasts without Him in our hearts. Our walk on earth is very short. We must get our priorities in order with Jesus to prepare for eternity in heaven. If you die today, which eternity will receive you - Heaven, which is Lightness or Hell which is Darkness? All you have to do is get down on your knees in prayer or bring your hands together in prayer and ask God for His guidance. He will fill your heart with His love and knowledge about life. Look what He has done for me!

During the editing stages of the book, Noell's (my wife's uncle) spiritual insight redirected me in a few things that I stated were wrong. One was that I stated we are all children of God. He is absolutely correct with pointing out that we are not all children of God, but created by God. We do not become children of God until we accept Jesus Christ as our Savior. The Bible verses below confirm the truth:

> But as many as received Him, to them He gave the right
> to become children of God, even to those who believe in
> His name, who were born not of blood, nor of the will
> of the flesh, nor the will of man, but of God.
>
>   John 1:12–13

It was interesting looking at synonyms for the words *spirit*, *light*, and *dark* which are as follows: Spirit is strength, courage, character, will, strength of mind and fortitude. *Light* is radiance, illumination and glow. *Dark* is dim, shady, gloomy and sinister. It only makes sense if we all would choose to live in spiritual lightness.

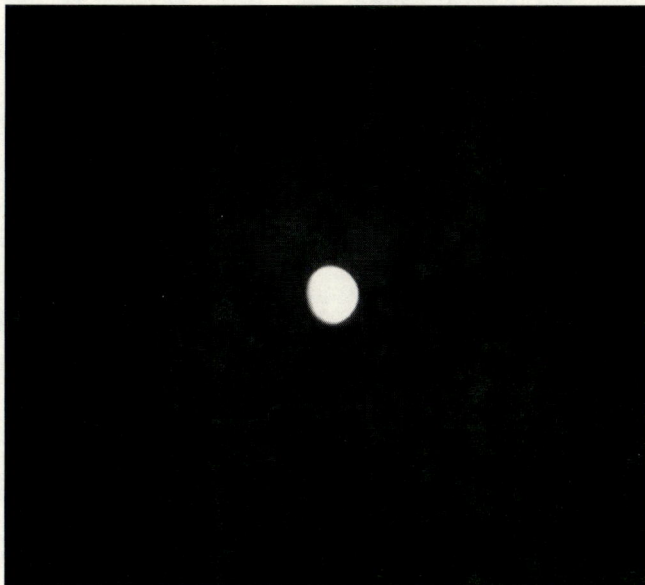

In the End Light will Prevail over Darkness
Moonlit Night

As a child, I remember seeing a commercial on television with a Cherokee Indian standing on a beautiful hillside looking down at a river and its banks. The old man had tears in his eyes as he watched the trash flowing with the water and accumulating on the riverbank. He remembered the days when his land was pristine, unspoiled - pure. I could understand why he had tears in his eyes. Look at how destructive we can be to our land and ourselves. Our sin can accumulate in our hearts just like trash accumulates on our river banks. I feel God is the same way when He looks down at us. He has tears in His eyes when we sin. I know He has had tears in His eyes for me. A sin is a sin whether we steal something that does not belong to us, we tell a lie, we are arrogant or boastful, we commit adultery, we murder someone, or we have a personal relationship with the same gender. The list could continue. The beauty of His forgiveness is He will forgive us for any sin we commit no matter how we dirty up ourselves. We just have to ask for His forgiveness. God wants all of us to become children of His and know Him as our heavenly Father. Accepting that Jesus died on the cross for us and asking for God's forgiveness is a new beginning in life.

I truly wonder where I would be in my spiritual life if Jesus had not appeared to me telling me I was His disciple. He placed it in my heart to share His story with you. He is what life is about. Jesus is real. God created us in His image so we would love and care for others. God is in our hearts; we just have to find Him. I don't know why He came to someone such as me because I fall so short of His glory, but He had faith that I would tell His story. When I get to heaven, I will thank Him for choosing me to deliver His word. You may also consider thanking God for your life. He does know you. I pray that you take my experience to your heart and it strengthens your faith to carry on.

Enter by the gate; for the gate is wide, and the way is broad that leads to destruction, and many are those who enter by it. For the gate is small, and the way is narrow that leads to life, and few are those who find it.
Matthew7:13–14

Then He will also say to those on His left, Depart from Me, accursed ones, into the eternal fire which has been

prepared for the devil and his angels; for I was hungry,
and you gave Me nothing to eat; I was thirsty, and you
gave Me nothing to drink; I was a stranger, and you
did not invite Me in; naked, and you did not clothe Me;
sick, and in prison, and you did not visit Me.

Matthew 25:41–43

I believe it is human nature to wonder why we are on earth and what we should be accomplishing in our lives. I have always hoped I could make a difference. I realize that I will soon be forgotten once I leave this earth. In reality, if we have children, they will carry what we taught them. They will remember us. If we are fortunate to have grandchildren, they will remember us also. A few friends, family members, and acquaintances will remember us. Then we are marked and remembered by only a headstone in a grave yard. What really matters in life is we must prepare ourselves for eternity. Life on earth is a temporary adventure versus eternity. Eternity is forever. I often feel inferior and still search to try to find my way while depending on myself, not depending on God for answers. This creates much turbulence and turmoil for me, and then I realize I only need to depend on God. With God's help I realized my number one priority is to treat people the way the Jesus would, with kindness and love. I realize I need to spend more time and energy focusing on His direction in life for me, not my own. This is what He wants us to do. As I reflect on my parents' lives, they did their best to teach me about our Lord; they were kind and cared for all people. They definitely accomplished God's purpose on earth. Life is not about OUR accomplishments on earth, but rather did we follow God's direction and meet His expectations as we grow as Christians.

When reading the book of Revelations, I found hope and warning. It talks of Jesus returning to earth to defeat Satan while God will reward the faithful with eternal life, and all who refuse to believe in him will face eternal punishment. The apocalyptic book and parts of it are most difficult to interpret. It has left me wondering if the Lord will come back to earth before I die. Often I think we will destroy ourselves through unrest, war, global warming, and other disparaging behavior we carry out by not following our Lord. Revelations chapter sixteen talks about every living thing in the sea dies, the land is scorched by the sun and the rivers run dry. After reading this I thought to myself we should really be concerned about pollution and its effects on our water supplies. Why is the Arctic rapidly melting; is the warming a natural occurrence or not? Water is a precious natural resource. We must have water to survive. I came to the realization that I cannot figure out what will happen in the future. I must be concerned about today, the moment and striving to walk with the Lord to make it to heaven–eternal life.

> *For the wages of sin is death, but the free gift of God is eternal life in Christ Jesus our Lord.*
>
> Romans 6:23

The other day I heard on the radio that in one state suicide was the leading cause of death, even more than homicides. When someone kills another, it is a terrible act because it shows that person does not value his or her own life, much less the lives of others. It is hard for me to understand how someone's heart has become so callous he or she is willing and able to take another's life. I do understand the desperate feelings of considering suicide, the feelings of losing hope for life. Since I was on the brink of committing suicide, I understand the depression and pain that can bring one to that point, and I feel great compassion when I hear that the suicide rate is increasing. I encourage anyone with thoughts of suicide to ask God's help during trying times and allow God to show you these tough times will pass. This issue will always penetrate my heart because when I was working with a corporate company a co-worker committed suicide. I missed opportunities to witness to him over a three-year period of time because he seemed distant. I believe it would have made a difference if I had talked to him about God, about life, not just about work. I missed an opportunity to strengthen someone's faith. We have many opportunities to share God's love with people. We must make the effort to share God's love; I must make the effort. It is too late to share our knowledge of the Lord with others after they have left this earth or even after we have left this earth.

Shortly before my dad left this earth to go to heaven, he wanted to talk about his life. He said that he felt he had not accomplished much in his life. I asked him what he meant by that. He said that he had not made a lot of money at his job and that he was not a wealthy man. I assured him that material wealth is not what life is about. I reminded him that he was loved by so many people, including his family. If one could put a monetary value on all the people that loved and cared for him, he would be a multi-billionaire. When we had his funeral, the church was filled to more than capacity. I often reflect on our talk and the relationships in my own life. Even though my dad made mistakes during his life, he truly should have peace in his heart since he left a positive footprint with people, friends, and family. He did love the Lord and treated people the way Jesus Christ did while on earth. His time on earth was not all about himself, but about being kind and giving to all. So many people miss this understanding about one's life when that person passes. There are those that can only recall the negative things a person has done. I truly hope I am like my dad when I leave this earth.

Faith

When I talk with people about heaven, often their response is they are not good enough to enter because they are sure they fall short of God's glory. We were not created perfect, so I understand their feelings of not being worthy. I believe that it is all about faith. We all fall short of God's glory. The Bible says that once we accept the gift Jesus gave us by dying on the cross for our sins, we have the faith to enter into heaven. The key, in my mind, is to live life as a disciple of Jesus. If you are not sure how strong your faith is, ask yourself this question, "If I face God tomorrow, will He allow me into heaven?" Your answer should be, "Yes, because Jesus Christ saved me." I have accepted Jesus as My Savior, and I have tried to walk with Jesus Christ in my life by being a disciple for Him, and sharing God's love. To stay in touch and have focus on our Lord, we must make prayer time a priority so He can guide us. Through prayer I experience the reality of Jesus and made the choice to live eternity in the light.

> *And He said to them, "Because of the littleness of your faith; truly I say to you, if you have faith as a mustard seed, you shall say to this mountain, 'Move from here to there,' and it shall move; and nothing shall be impossible to you.*
>
> Matthew 17:20

One of the hardest things for many of us is to place our faith in something that we cannot touch or see. Our world today calls for scientific evidence and lawful witness which discounts "faith." Jesus addressed the same issues by saying, "You saw and did not believe–blessed are those who did not see, but believed!" Growing up in church I was encouraged by the power of the Bible stories, yet I could never grasp that I needed to accept God's love like I accepted the love of my earthly parents. Often our minds are in turmoil trying to figure out the complex spiritual concept of appreciating and loving our heavenly Father. Some, it seems, as God pierces their hearts in a gentle way easily accept His love and walk in faith. I for one had to be in a desperate situation to see the need to accept His love. Only when I accepted His love could I understand the truth about life, and the way I should live my life. There are others that never accept His love because their spirit is too preoccupied with worldly adventures. We do not know the date or the moment we will face eternity; however, no matter what journey we take in life, our final destination is eternity.

A friend sent the following to me by email: "The road to success is not straight[9]. There is a curve called Failure, a loop called Confusion, speed bumps called Friends, red lights called Enemies, caution lights called Family. You will have flats called Jobs. But, if you have a spare called Determination, an engine called Perseverance, insurance called Faith, a driver called Jesus, you will make it to a place called Success."

As I reflected on the words, they resembled my walk on earth. I realized since I accepted Jesus' love, grace and power into my life I have been able to deal with adversity better. Through Jesus, God gives us insight to why we make mistakes and why others actions sometimes brings us difficulties. Carrying the Lord in my heart has brought me more wisdom and insight; my life has been better knowing Jesus Christ.

> *Now faith is the assurance of things hoped for, the conviction of things not seen. By faith we understand that the worlds were prepared by the word of God, so that what is seen was not made out of things which are visible.*
>
> Hebrews 11:1, 3

> *But, Jesus, overhearing what was being spoken, said to the synagogue official, "Do not be afraid any longer, only believe."*
>
> Mark 5:36

Thoughts for Reflection

- If we learn to live life each day as if it were our last, I bet we could get much more out of life.

- We face many experiences in our lives, good and bad. Some of the bad we bring to ourselves, some are brought on by others, and some just happen. This is life. If we walk with the Lord, we can get through and learn from our experiences.

- God will come to us many times during our lifetime. When this happens, take time to reflect on your life and make a decision to ask for His love and guidance. You may not be here tomorrow to make the decision.

- Life on earth is temporary. We waste so much of our energy holding onto anger, guilt, and resentment while striving for material things and wishing for approval of others. We must stop wasting our energy on trivial stuff. We need to take time to love ourselves then we can care for others. The only way I have found to truly like myself is through the love of the Lord.

- Often I find myself depending on God only when I am at a low point in my life. As I reflect on my life, I need to depend on Him daily for His direction.

- Build others up; do not try to destroy them with words. This should apply in relationships with others, directing and teaching our children, etc.

- Unfortunately we often do not take advice, direction, and wisdom from others when making choices. We do not listen to or depend on God for His guidance. We have to learn the hard way—from our mistakes!

- While writing this book, I have been diligent to complete the work. I have dreamed that my story would become a number one selling book or just sell enough copies to feel it was a success! Often we do not know if our hard work will lead us to success. After reflecting on my effort, I hope only that God's story through me will change a few hearts.

- The most important thing we need to remember in our daily walk is how Jesus would react to each situation we face and how He would have treated people that came across His path. If we try to act as He did, we will become better people. Amen.

Bible Verses for Study

And He was passing through from one city and village to another, teaching, and proceeding on His way to Jerusalem. And someone said to Him, "Lord, are there just a few who are being saved?" And he said to them, "Strive to enter by the narrow door; for many, I tell you, will seek to enter and will not be able. "Once the head of the house gets up and shuts the door, and you begin to stand outside and knock on the door, saying 'Lord, open up to us!' then He will answer and say to you, 'I do not know where you are from.' Then you will begin to say, 'We ate and drank in Your presence, and You taught our streets'; and He will say, 'I tell

you, I do not know where you are from; DEPART
FROM ME, ALL EVILDOERS.'

Luke 13:22–27

The Mighty One, God, the Lord, has spoken, And
summoned the earth from the rising of the sun to its
setting. Out of Zion, the perfection of beauty, God has
shone forth. May our God come and not keep silence;
Fire devours before Him, And it is very tempestuous
around Him. He summons the heavens above, And
the earth, to judge His people; "Gather My godly ones
to Me, Those who have made a covenant with Me by
sacrifice." And the heavens declare His righteousness.
For God Himself is judge.

Psalm 50:1–6

"But in those days, after that tribulation, the sun
will be darkened, and the moon will not give any its
light, And the stars will be falling from heaven, and
the powers that are in the heavens will be shaken.
"And then they will see the Son of Man coming in
clouds with great power and glory. "And then He
will send forth the angels, and will gather together
His elect from the four winds, from the farthest end
of the earth, to the farthest end of heaven.

Mark 13:24–27

Never pay back evil for evil to anyone. Respect
what is right in the sight of all men. If possible,
so far as it depends on you, be at peace with all
men. Never take your own revenge, beloved, but
leave room for the wrath of God, for it is written,
"Vengeance is Mine, I will repay," says the Lord.

Romans 13:17–19

By faith they passed through the Red Sea as though they were passing through dry land; and the Egyptians, when they attempted it, drowned.

Hebrews 11:29

And Jesus was going about in all Galilee, teaching in their synagogues, and proclaiming the gospel of the kingdom, and healing every kind of disease and every kind of sickness among the people.

Matthew 5:23

"For if you forgive men for their transgressions, your heavenly Father will also forgive you. "But if you do not forgive men, then your heavenly father will not forgive your transgressions.

Matthew 6:14

And when the disciples saw Him walking on the sea, they were frightened, saying, "It is a ghost!" And they cried out for fear. But immediately Jesus spoke to them, saying, "Take courage, it is I; do not be afraid." And Peter answered Him and said, "Lord, if it is You, command me to come to You on the water." And He said, "Come!" And Peter got out of the boat, and walked on the water and came toward Jesus. But seeing the wind, he became afraid, and beginning to sink, he cried out, saying, "Lord, save me!" And immediately Jesus stretched out His hand and took hold of him, and said to him, "O you of little faith, why did you doubt?"

Matthew 14:26–31

Not that I have already obtained it, or have already become perfect, but I press on in order that I may lay hold of that for which also I was laid hold of by Christ Jesus. Brethren I do not regard myself as having laid hold of it yet; but one thing I do: forgetting what lies behind and reaching forward to what is ahead, I press on toward the goal for the prize of the upward call of God in Christ Jesus.

Philippians 3:12–14

BEHOLD, the Lord's hand is not so short that it cannot save; Neither is His ear so dull That it cannot hear. But your iniquities have made a separation between you and your God, And your sins have hidden His face from you, so that He does not hear.

Isaiah 59:1–2

Consider it all joy, my brethren, when you encounter various trials, knowing that the testing of your faith produces endurance. And let endurance have its perfect result, that you may be perfect and complete, lacking in nothing. But if any of you lacks wisdom, let him ask of God, who gives to all men generously and without reproach, and it will be given to him. But let him ask in faith without any doubting, for the one who doubts is like the surf of the sea driven and tossed by the wind.

James 1:2–6

Questions

1. Does God want us to hurt or get hurt on this earth? Please explain your answer.

2. Why does hard work, dedication/applying ourselves in everything we do pay off in the end?

3. Should we blame God for sending a hurricane such as Katrina that destroyed the Gulf Coast or should we just use more caution in making decisions to minimize danger by not building in a flood zone of a coastal area where we know hurricanes create devastation?

4.   Do you have peace and contentment in your life? If so,
     what brought you to that point?

5.   When you cross the finish line at the end of your life, will
     you be in heaven? If your answer is yes, please explain
     how you know this.

6.   If you do not have the Lord in your life, upon what do
     you base your values?

7.   Why is important to be a disciple for the Lord?

God's Plan

I realized through writing this book other authors have written books about how to become a better person, to love yourself, to change your spirit, and live life to your full potential. A few of the books have become number one sellers because so many people are searching to find answers and purpose in their lives. People are searching for ways to be content, to be happy, so that they can enjoy life. The older we get, we become more concerned about death—we become more concerned about eternity. Unfortunately from some people's perspective, they tell us we can get to heaven by just being a good person, and feeling good about ourselves. The truth is God tells us the only way to Him is through His son Jesus Christ.

Jesus said to him, I am the way, and the truth, and the life; no one comes to the Father, but through Me. If you had known Me, you would have known My Father also; from now on you know Him, and have seen Him.

John 14:6–7

And many false prophets will arise, and will mislead many.

Matthew 24:11

Then the Lord said to me, "The prophets are prophesying falsehood in My name. I have neither sent them nor commanded them nor spoken to them; they are prophesying to you a false vision, divination, futility and deception of their own minds.

Jeremiah 14:14

Who is the liar but the one who denies that Jesus is the Christ? This is the antichrist, the one who denies the Father and the Son.

I John 2:22

My hope is this book will guide you to the only book that can build a spiritual foundation in your life, the Bible. God created us in His image; therefore, He has set eternity in our hearts. This means we can never be completely satisfied with earthly pleasures. Before we can begin this journey into the light, we need to realize and accept what Jesus actually did on the cross for us. He died on the cross for each one of us. We need to let this understanding permeate (saturate) our hearts. Only then can we begin to understand our spiritual purpose. We need God the

Father and Jesus Christ His son in our lives to become a better person, to be content, to bring happiness within our spirit and to enjoy life to its fullest.

> *Therefore we have been buried with Him through baptism into death, in order that as Christ was raised from the dead through the glory of the Father, so we too might walk in newness of life. For if we have become united in the likeness of His death, certainly we shall be also in the likeness of His resurrection, knowing this, that our old self was crucified with Him, that our body of sin might be done away with, that we should no longer be slaves to sin; for he who has died is freed from sin. Now if we have died with Christ, we believe that we shall also live with Him, knowing that Christ, having been raised from the dead, is never to die again; death no longer is master over Him. For the death that He died, He died to sin, once for all: but the life that He lives, He lives to God. Even so consider yourselves to be dead to sin, but alive to God in Christ Jesus.*
>
> Romans 5:4–11

In order to become a better person, we must lose sight of ourselves and focus on the way Jesus walked on earth. Often verses from the Bible talk about self-control, self-will, self-centeredness and selfishness. Our minds naturally want to lead us in spiritual darkness which centers our focus toward ourselves which leads us to discontentment; we are never satisfied. God gives us the freedom to choose the life we lead. He does not demand us to live in spiritual *light*. He allows our hearts to accept or not accept His peace and love. Satan would prefer us not to accept the truth of Jesus Christ. If you choose the Lord in your life, this does not indicate you are weak, but that you have matured as an individual and are strong for doing so.

> *For men will be lovers of self, lovers of money, boastful, arrogant, revilers, disobedient to parents, ungrateful, unholy, unloving, irreconcilable, malicious gossips, without self-control, brutal, haters of good, treacherous, reckless, conceited lovers of pleasure rather than lovers of God.*
>
> II Timothy 3:2–4

God wants us to enjoy life knowing He is always near to calm us with His presence. Often we pursue our goals with the wrong intentions. Much of the time we know what we should do or the way we should act, but do not. We waste so much energy and time feeling guilty, holding onto resentment, being angry, carrying fear, wanting approval, worrying about big or small issues on the horizon, and thinking of things we want to do or acquire. We often go off in many different directions, trying to find happiness and contentment. Deep in our souls we know what could make us happy, but do nothing about it. Why do we not change? God wants us to enjoy our gifts, but we must recognize the gifts are from Him. The first commandment tells us to place God first in our lives. When we accept God into our lives, He brings us new ideas as how to address issues that arises in our daily living. His spiritual direction and ways are much better than our old ways. My old ways sure did not bring me peace and solid direction.

We need to realize life on earth is temporary; wasting our lives on trivial issues is pointless. Often life may seem unfair to us. When this happens, we need to stay focused on God. Driven by spiritual purpose for the Lord is what is needed in our lives. We should focus on the path God wants us to take, His direction. When we take His direction, good things will occur normally. I state "normally" because life does have it peaks and valleys even with God in our lives, but He promises to never leave us. When we do not truly listen to God or we have friends who do not have common Christian beliefs, life can become difficult. Through our faith God does give us hope for a better day. In the end He gives us eternal life in heaven with Him.

Who among you is wise and understanding? Let him show by his good behavior his deeds in the gentleness of wisdom. But if you have a bitter jealousy and self ambition in your heart, do not be arrogant and so lie against the truth. This wisdom is not that which comes down from above, but is earthly, natural, demonic. For where jealousy and self ambition exist, there is disorder and every evil thing. But the wisdom from above is first pure, then peaceable, gentle, reasonable, full of mercy and good fruits, unwavering, without hypocrisy. And the seed whose fruit is righteousness is sown in peace by those who make peace.

James 3:13–18

For this is the covenant that I will make with the house of Israel. After those days says the Lord: I will put My laws into their minds, And I will write them upon their hearts. And I will be their God, And they shall be My people.

Hebrews 8:10

Since therefore, brethren, we have confidence to enter the holy place by the blood of Jesus, by a new and living way which He inaugurated for us through the veil, that is, His flesh and since we have a great priest over the house of God, let us draw near with a sincere heart in full assurance of faith, having our hearts sprinkled clean from an evil conscience and our bodies washed with pure water. Let us hold fast the confession of our hope without wavering, for He who promised is faithful; and let us consider how to stimulate one another to love and good deeds, not forsaking our own assembling together, as is the habit of some, but encouraging one another; and all the more, as you see the day drawing near.

Hebrews 10:19–25

Being darkened in their understanding, excluded from life of God, because of the ignorance that is in them, because of the hardness of their heart; and they having become callous, have given themselves over to sensuality, for the practice of every kind of impurity with greediness. But you did not learn Christ in this way.

Ephesians 4:18–20

The Lord lift up His countenance on you, And give you peace.

Numbers 6:26

The Lord will give strength to His people; The Lord will bless His people with peace.

Psalm 29:11

Consider what I say, for the Lord will give you understanding in everything.

II Timothy 2:7

Are You or a Family Member Looking for Love and Peace in Life?

For you were formerly darkness, but now you are light in the Lord; walk as children of light (for the fruit of the light consists in all goodness and righteousness and truth), trying to learn what is pleasing to the Lord.

Ephesians 5:8–10

I waited patiently for the Lord; And He inclined to me and heard my cry. He brought me up out of the pit of destruction, out of the miry clay; And He set my feet upon a rock making my footsteps firm. And He put a new song in my mouth, a song of praise to our God; Many will see and fear, And will trust in the Lord. How blessed is the man who has made the Lord his trust. And has not turned to the proud, nor to those who lapse into falsehood.

Psalm 40:1–4

Once I accepted the Lord's love, He gave me a new outlook toward life. The little things that I took for granted such as seeing a beautiful sunset or the seasons changing from summer to fall when the leaves in the mountains magnified their beautiful colors were even more magnificent after I found the Lord's love, peace, wisdom, and strength. I appreciated the simple things in life even more. I was amazed that He could create something so beautiful. Things that I perceived as important lost their meaning. The simple things in life began to mean more to me than buying material possessions. Once I found God the Father, Jesus the Son, and the Holy Spirit I realized that I should be more like Jesus while on earth. Jesus' focus on earth was to reveal God to man, turn hearts to God, reveal sin and provide salvation.

As a Christian, our main objective should be that we are disciples for the Lord, to share our knowledge and experiences with strangers, with friends, and with family. Our mission as a parent should be that we disciple our children to see Jesus in us, teach them His ways, and help them find their God-given gifts. The purposes of this story are to share with you my experience when Jesus Christ appeared to me and also the power of His love. I pray that everyone who reads this book can feel His presence and feel Him calling his or her name. If you did not feel His presence, please go back and read "The Appearance" chapter again. Close your eyes; then say, "Jesus, let me understand." It will happen if you open your heart to Him.

> As in water face reflects man. So the heart of man reflects man.
>
> Proverbs 27:19

> Let your light shine before men in such a way that they may see your good works, and glorify your Father who is in heaven.
>
> Matthew 5:16

We should place the verse below into our hearts and think of it often as a reminder about our walk on earth toward eternity. This is one of the verses that I began with in the introduction. It has a profound meaning to me since Jesus appeared to me as a vapor and vanished after He spoke. It was an awesome and remarkable experience! In one way, we are no different than Jesus—we are here on earth for a little while and are gone tomorrow for eternity. Jesus may or may not appear to you on this earth as He did to me. I truly pray that you take my experience with Jesus to your heart, believe, and He will "Appear" to you in some way.

Yet you do not know what your life will be like tomorrow. You are just a vapor that appears for a little while and then vanishes away. Instead, you ought to say, "If the Lord wills, we shall live and also do this or that." But as it is, you boast in your arrogance; all such boasting is evil.

James 4:14–16

Once I found Jesus I realized that He was perfect. God gave me insight to the perfection of His creation–Jesus His son. He gave me understanding, but I cannot see into the future or comprehend *all* of His plans. I have come to the point I just need to do His work on earth by being a disciple while having my sights on eternal life in the light with Him. There are so many things that God has planned for us; one that really hits home with me is death. We do not know when our lives on earth will end. We need to be spiritually prepared for eternity.

There is appointed time for everything. And there is a time for every event under heaven—

A time to give birth, and a time to die;
A time to plant, and a time to uproot what is planted.
A time to kill, and a time to heal;
A time to tear down, and a time to build up.
A time to weep, and a time to laugh;
A time to mourn, and a time to dance.
A time to throw stones, and a time to gather stones;
A time to embrace, and a time to shun embracing,
A time to search, and a time to give up as lost;
A time to keep, and a time to throw away.

A time to tear apart, and a time to sew together;
A time to be silent, and a time to speak.
A time to love, and a time to hate.
A time for war, and a time for peace.

What profit is there to the worker from that he toils?
I have seen the task which God has given the sons of
men with which to occupy themselves. He has made
everything appropriate in its time. He has also set
eternity in their heart, yet so that man will not find
out the work which God has done from the beginning
even to the end. I know that there is nothing better for
them than to rejoice and to do good in one's lifetime;

Ecclesiastes 3:1–12

Through my study and spiritual growth, I realize I am not perfect. I will never be perfect. I will not always make the right decisions, and I have issues that I need to overcome with the Lord's help. This is quite humbling to know that I cannot achieve perfection in this present body. One of the hardest things to do in my life is to forgive myself and to forgive someone for hurting me, a friend or family member. As I have grown with the Lord, He has given me the power to forgive a person. Why should I forgive someone? Because Jesus forgives me for my sins, I should do the same for someone else. It may take me a day, a month, or more to overcome the hurt that was caused. It is amazing the peace the Lord gives us in tough situations such as forgiving someone. It seems that once I work through to forgiveness, I realize I feel sorrow for that person because in most cases, they are missing the Lord in their lives. Where would I be without the Lord in my life? Through my walk in life, I realized *if* I stay focused on the Lord daily, I become a better person. Along our life paths we need to stay focused on our Lord. He will give us His plan, and we must listen and follow Him. Do not merely exist on earth. Live with the joy and peace that the Lord can place in your heart.

> *I am the door; if anyone enters through Me, he shall be saved, and shall go in and out, and find pasture. The thief comes only to steal, and kill, and destroy; I come that they might have life, and might have it abundantly. I am the good shepherd; the good shepherd lays down His life for the sheep.*
>
> John 10:9–11
>
> *And that be renewed in the spirit of your mind, and put on the new self, which in the likeness of God has been created in righteousness and holiness of the truth.*
>
> Ephesians 4:23–24

> *The Lord is my shepherd, I shall not want. He makes me lie down in green pastures; He leads me beside quiet waters. He restores my soul; He guides me in the paths of righteousness For His name's sake. Even though I walk through the valley of the shadow of death, I fear no evil; for Thou art with me; Thy rod and Thy staff, they comfort me. Thou dost prepare a table before me in the presence of my enemies. Thou hast anointed my head with oil; My cup overflows. Surely goodness and loving kindness will follow me all the days of my life, And I will dwell in the house of the Lord forever.*
>
> Psalm 23:1–6

During a time of emotional suffering I found Jesus. I realized, reflecting on my life, I had opportunities to hear Him and accept His love when I was younger, but had chosen not to. He has taught me so much about life, and I believe He wants me to share my story with you in the hope that you will be able to avoid some of the mistakes I made. Being a Christian is like taking a long walk that never ends until your life on earth ends. It is a lifetime of learning and growing in an endeavor to become a person more like the image of Jesus. As long as one listens to his or her heart and stays focused on His teachings, the strength to persevere will become part of your life. It is not a cakewalk. Man, by nature, has a tendency toward self-centeredness and the desire to be in control. That is the challenge one must overcome to walk with Jesus. Change is hard because one has to leave behind what has been comfortable. Change begins with knowing God. Jesus stated the greatest commandment is, "You shall love the Lord your God with all your heart, and with all your soul, and with all your mind." Change begins with knowing Jesus. Each successful day is a blessing, and a prayer of thanks to the Lord for each day brings one closer to his or her goal to be like Jesus. Be thankful for your time on earth because it is short and you do not know when the Lord will call you or a loved one home.

Thoughts for Reflection

- God opens our minds and awakens our spirit to new things. If your old ways are not working, try something different. If we listen, we can learn; if we open our hearts, we can change. If you do not have the Lord in your heart, take the time to invite Him in. Don't wait until tomorrow to ask. Tomorrow may not be there for you on this earth.

- Do not judge someone else. We need to worry about ourselves on Judgment Day.

- Life on earth is short. Eternity is forever. Choose the love of Jesus Christ and heaven.

- If you are searching for a purpose in your life, it could be that you are missing the Lord in your life.

- We face various trials during our walk in life. Focus on the Lord; keep your faith. We will endure with Him.

- Remember it is never too late to accept Jesus Christ as your Savior. The criminal hanging on the cross next to Jesus accepted Him minutes before he died, and Jesus promised him a place in heaven. We are no different.

- Therefore, become a person of wisdom and gain contentment and the abundant life available to all who walk in the admonition of the Lord. Prevail and overcome through acknowledgment and understanding of the plan Jesus Christ has for you.

Questions

I stated early in the book that the Bible alone answers the greatest questions we face during our lives. Please answer the following:

1.   How can I know the truth about life?

2.   What happens when we die if we live in the Spirit of the Light?

3.   Psalm 23:1 states "The Lord is my Shepherd"; what is the responsibility of a Shepherd?

4.   What happens when we die if we live in the Spirit of Darkness?

5.   What are God's greatest two commandments to us?

6. What kind of fruit are you producing in your life?

7. What is God's purpose for us in our life?

8. How can difficult times in our lives make us stronger?

9. How do we learn what God's plan is for us?

10. Why is it important to share our godly experiences and
    what we have learned from our failures with others?

11. Today, what spirit are you carrying in your heart?

12. What changes can you make in your life to become more like Jesus?

Endnotes

1. The Merriam-Webster Dictionary, "Jealousy"
2. The Merriam-Webster Dictionary, "Disciple"
3. Wikipedia–the Free Encyclopedia (en.wikipedia.org)
4. The Merriam-Webster Dictionary, "Discipline"
5. The Life Application Bible, New International Version edition, "Book of Proverbs Megathemes"
6. The Merriam-Webster Dictionary, "Success"
7. The Life Application Bible, New International Version edition, "Book of Ecclesiastes Megathemes"
8. The Merriam-Webster Dictionary, "Vanity"
9. "Unknown Author, "The road to success is not straight."